# Making It Rain

# A Study of High Performing Sales People in Law, Accountancy and Financial Services

*by Simon Bozeat*

"Making it Rain identifies succinctly the critical success factors that differentiate the great professional service firms from the good. It proves in no uncertain terms why solicitors, accountants and others in professional service firms must adopt a commercial focus first and a process focus second."

**Tim Moore**
**Financial Director**
**Vision Express**
\*\*\*\*

"I think the report is an excellent platform for change. I look forward to using it as benchmarking tool to help engage in a quality debate on what we do well and what we have to do to improve our marketing and business development performance."

**Carley Ferguson**
**Marketing Manager**
**Harvey Ingram LLP**
\*\*\*\*

"This is a very well researched and thorough document. It makes us realise that there is so much more to learn and so much more we should be doing. Some readers may rightly be unsettled by the breadth and depth of the business development issues facing our profession. This report will light the spark that creates the motivation to do something about them."

**Mike Copestake**
**Senior Partner**
**Freeth Cartwright Solicitors**
\*\*\*\*

"10/10! It is scarily accurate. A broad and incisive reflection of the challenges facing my profession."

**Chris Britton-Powell**

**Principal**
**Lawyers4IT**
\*\*\*\*

"Throughout the development of my practice we have and will continue to work for our clients throughout the UK in partnership with solicitors and accountants from large and small firms. There are many vital messages contained in 'Making it Rain' for all of us who work in the professional services sector. It is increasingly crucial for service professionals to have both the will and skill to form solid relationships based on trust, integrity and outstanding service with clients, colleagues and partners. This report highlights this explicitly and shows you what to do to move from a traditional profession led firm to a thriving and profitable sales and service led business."

**Steven Hewitt**
**Partner**
**80Twenty Financial Services**
\*\*\*\*

"Making it Rain is a thought-provoking and challenging piece of research. It is full of nuggets of wisdom and common sense suggestions for increasing our own rainmaking powers and bringing on the next generation of rainmakers. Simon Bozeat argues persuasively that in the modern professional services world, we ignore this at our peril."

**Mark Hacking**
**Partner, Commercial Dispute Resolution**
**Geldards LLP**
**Nottingham**
\*\*\*\*

# Table of Contents

# Introduction

What are the factors that contribute to or inhibit sales success in professional service firms?

This is the question at the heart of the research project. The decision to carry out this research was prompted by three events:

1. This book is the result of a research project that was conducted into the habits of top 'Rainmakers' – The business networking professionals who generate business. Over 200 networking events were attended and the behaviours that differentiated average and accomplished networkers were noted. This led to the development of the acclaimed 'Working the Net' book and a highly acclaimed training programme "How to Build a Profitable Business Network". Lawyers, accountants and financial services professionals were observed. Many were good, a few true masters and sadly the majority were largely putting in a lot of effort and time with minimal reward.

2. Since being in business many good friends, who work in the professional services, have shared valuable insights into these professions.

3. Many of our past and present clients work in professional services. We have had the good fortune to coach one-to-one many top producers in financial services who are continuously looking for the edge to bring them into contact with seriously wealthy people. They have all had interesting opinions about people working in law and accounting.

The main focus of this research has been in law and accountancy; however we have spoken to many people in financial services, banking and other professional service firms who tell us that the conclusions are equally applicable to these sectors.

The research has encompassed one comprehensive study of a highly successful and profitable law firm plus 31 interviews with partners, senior partners, HR professionals, heads of marketing and fee earners in other firms. The research included interviews with representatives from 40% of the top city of London accounting firms and one of the so called 'Big 4'.

This research comprised of 4 phases:

**Phase I**

We asked a select group of people for their answers to the primary question. **"What are the factors that contribute to and inhibit sales success in professional service firms?"**

This revealed a series of factors and their negative and positive consequences. This was compiled into a four-page document which formed the basis of the interviews (Appendix 1). The interviewees were asked to provide their honest and open opinions on how and whether these factors and their consequences applied to them and if so to what extent. Each interview lasted between 26 and 59 minutes.

This led to the following conclusions:

- Customers believe that when they do business with a law or accountancy firm the people they instruct are qualified to do the job they are paying for.
- Accountants and solicitors have a relatively high IQ.
- Firms are often organised into partnerships.
- Law and accountancy firms are in a very competitive market.
- Firms cannot rely on their professionalism and expertise to maintain their business growth.
- There are some examples of best practice in sales and marketing but to an extent as a profession they are playing catch up to other comparable service industries.
- There is, to a large extent, reluctance on the part of many partners and fee earners to embrace new ways of selling themselves and the firm.

- Some small and large firms are embracing new ways of working and are stealing significant chunks of the market.

## Phase II

The second phase of the research pulled the findings together into a set of 30 generic business development challenges that professional service firms face. These are given in appendix 2. Unsurprisingly, to date, not one organisation has said they are consistently addressing all the challenges.

The main conclusions were as follows:

**Important note!**
Please bear in mind the general nature of these conclusions. Generalisations are, by definition, not always true and are therefore not applicable to all businesses and all parts of the professions.

1. Financial services seemed to have embraced modern sales and marketing methods ahead of accountancy and accountancy is ahead of law.

2. In the preliminary research we listed a series of factors that we believed would be true. However not one of the factors and their consequences was consistently accepted as true for all the respondents. There were, however, some trends. These are listed throughout this document.

3. There are a series of paradoxes within the industries. These are listed throughout this document.

4. The majority of professional service firms are only scratching the surface of the enormous potential that lies in adopting advanced business development and marketing techniques.

5. The majority of firms recognise that there are huge reservoirs of budding Rainmakers whose talent and potential has yet to be unleashed.

6. There are a plethora of unhelpful beliefs about lawyers and accountants shared by the public, customers and the professions.

7. Whilst significant effort is being made to differentiate firms in the marketplace, less attention is placed on creating a vibrant, creative and fun place for people to work.

8. 98% of the people we contacted were very interested in this research. When asked why, it became clear that each firm was facing some serious business development challenges.

9. The relative volume and quality of non-technical training and education and expertly delivered coaching activity is paltry.

## Phase III

Phase three of the research was to develop this report which discloses the insights, stories, conclusions and options for creating the next generation of Rainmakers.

## Phase IV

This is a process to collect quantitative data about the 30 challenges. Decision makers are being invited to complete the 30 challenge self assessment form for their business to reveal statistical evidence to support the conclusions. Phase IV will continue for decades.

# Using The Book

There are 16 chapters. Each chapter has a series of headings, either a title or a key question. There will be a description of the issue including some anecdotes and quotes, all are based on genuine conversations although some of the names, by request, have been withheld or changed.

Some of the themes in the chapters overlap. For example it is difficult to totally separate sales, marketing and service.

My company is one specialising in training and coaching. Consequently attention has been placed primarily on the human element of sales success. Less focus has been paid to systems, organisation and pay, although some observations have been included. One of the goals of this report is to challenge some unhelpful myths about the role of training and coaching in bringing about massive, positive and sustained change to a business.

In some of the chapters there are some specific recommendations; in others the issues are wider and more generic.

In appendix 10 we cover a little about why my company exists and what we do. The reason this is included is to demonstrate some of the underlying principles and beliefs that have driven the focus of the report. In appendix 3 we have listed 11 options you might like to consider for your business. These are designed to help you develop the next generation of Rainmakers. Many of the original contributors have already used the 30 challenges to quickly pinpoint specific areas where they need to improve their business.

## A health warning!

Prior to publishing the report we sent it to a dozen of the original contributors for analysis and comment. Several contributors warned us about the readers reacting adversely to some of the inflammatory language used in parts of the report. We were advised to make it just factual as the majority of accountants and lawyers have highly developed left brains (analysis and logic). They would therefore rebel against any emotive language. We were also advised that we should not make any negative references that could be construed as an attack on the professions.

We thanked them for their advice and chose, rightly or wrongly (you will be the judge), to do exactly the opposite and keep it all in.

These are the 7 reasons behind this decision:

1. The emotive language was used by the contributors. All we have done is replicate what we were told.

2. If, at any stage while you are reading the report, you find yourself getting frustrated or even annoyed at the content, good! This means the facts are causing you to feel uncomfortable and we know that pain is a prerequisite to any change.

3. We were advised to remove all the comments based on people's gender. One contributor was adamant we should take out all references to women. Again we thought long and hard about the impact of leaving them in. We decided to do so as, if we followed the advice and left them out, it would be unfair to the other contributors who gave us their valuable time and opinions.

4. If, at any stage, you find yourself getting defensive, this is an indication that there is part of you that needs to drop its guard and allow you to receive and respond to feedback and new ideas.

5. Master Rainmakers have highly developed left and right brains, they are open-minded to ideas and actively seek new ways of doing business.

6. Master Rainmakers know that the majority of people buy on emotion and justify their decision on logic.

7. We have tried our very best to keep the report balanced. We know change is as much about moving from a painful place as it is pursuing a compelling vision.

Consequently, in our opinion, the final chapter 'Can you skate anti-clockwise?' is the most important. However, for many readers it will be the greatest challenge to relate to and absorb.

A final note for readers who practice in smaller firms. The emphasis of the research has been in medium to large businesses; however there are many simple strategies and tips contained throughout the report applicable to any firm irrespective of its size. There is a chapter towards the end of the report which covers several lessons from the larger firms specifically for micro businesses.

We trust you find the results of the research informative and thought- provoking. Many of the original contributors and clients are already using it both as a way to help prevent mistakes others have made and as a stimulus for making a difference to their organisations.

Simon Bozeat

# 1: The Paradoxes

Here are 5 of the more interesting paradoxes discovered during the research. There are many others throughout the report.

### 1. Financial services v accountancy/law

The recent highly publicised disclosures of mis-selling of financial services have done the image of the profession no favours at all. Regulation and an increasing emphasis on becoming qualified to sell products has gone a long way to address this. However, in the eyes of many lawyers and accountants, IFA's (Independent Financial Advisors) and tied agents are not in the same league. The paradox is that many of these professionals have made significant strides in their marketing and selling activities and become extremely sophisticated. So who is going to learn from whom?

When we highlighted this to one contributor, a Master Rainmaker, he correctly pointed out that that the majority of people in financial services identify themselves as salespeople and are trained to sell yet many solicitors and accountants are not. Indeed one contributor told us that the reason many people are drawn to the professions is so they don't have to talk to people! This is one of the key challenges budding Rainmakers face, simply believing that they can be one.

### 2. Technical v sales skills

Clients will believe that a solicitor or accountant will be able to competently do their job. Educational institutions and firms invest significant amounts of time and effort to ensure their people are technically qualified. However, from a business development perspective the key differentiator is normally the quality of the relationship not technical skill. Yet the amount of time and resources put into training lawyers and accountants in people skills e.g. creating rapport, how to understand what motivates/demotivates individual clients, matching language patterns and personal presentation, is relatively and pitifully small.

Marc McCormack, the late founder of IMG and originally a lawyer, believed that success in law was less about the practice of law and more about personality and people.

### 3.  Caution v boldness

The professions rightly breed detail-conscious and risk-averse people who are cautious and adopt a 'Ready, ready, ready, aim, fire' approach.
However the competitive world demands that people move outside of their comfort zones to become more entrepreneurial and try new sales and marketing strategies. This often requires a bold, 'Ready, Fire, Aim' approach.

### 4.  Individuality v teamwork

Top service professionals will build intimate relationships with their customers based on being highly professional, listening and doing a great job. Customers will often follow an individual irrespective of which firm he/she works for. This intimacy can breed protectionism and a reluctance to introduce clients to colleagues.

Firms with large organisations as clients understand the importance of sharing contacts and working in cross-department teams to effectively manage accounts. The introduction and consistent use of account management methodology and systems is essential to deliver exceptional service and manage all the many contacts that occur between the firm and the client.

This requires a shift in mindset often indicated simply by the switch in phraseology from *'my client'* to *'our client.'* Very few of the respondents stated that protectionism was not an issue. Interestingly one of these was a publicly owned company.

### 5.  Use and abuse of power

One of the research questions investigated whether lawyers and accountants used their position and power with clients wisely. It is clear that there are many opportunities to influence clients yet this privileged position in the inner circles carries the risk of over inflating the ego. The potential consequence is to stop listening hard for sales opportunities. Few of the respondents could put their finger on how power was abused in terms of winning or losing business. However there were many comments about how awful some of the partners are in abusing their position when managing people!

Many of our friends in financial services, who are genuine experts in their field, find themselves pulling their hair out when they are presenting a compelling case to a client. Whilst the client may be taken by the prospect of saving vast sums in tax or generating significant returns from investments, when they refer the proposal to their accountant, it is sometimes blocked. The IFA or tied agent is perhaps seen by some accountants as a threat and the proposal is dismissed without a full appreciation of the detail. In the eyes of the IFA the accountant may not be in a position to offer good advice to the client due to a lack of knowledge in the subject matter. The result is a lose/lose situation.

Now before all the accountants reading this shout 'foul!' it is also our experience that there are many open-minded, professional and highly qualified accountants who do not share any of these traits. We also say that our own perceptions of the financial services profession have radically changed. Years ago, in our eyes, they were considered very unprofessional. Our view is now the opposite; some of our clients in financial services are amongst the best salespeople we have had the pleasure and privilege to meet, train and coach.

# 2: 80% of success is in the mind

## 2.1 Mindset

In the early 90s we were shown diagram (a) by Robin Fielder, a sales guru, at one of his big motivational events 'Close that Sale'. This was intended to reveal the characteristics of a top salesperson. We held onto this view for many years until we began to challenge its validity. The ingredients are right but the proportions are not. As a consulting practice we believe that success is determined by diagram (b). Having the right mindset is essential for anyone who wishes to rise to the top, irrespective of the profession they choose to pursue.

Diagram (a)                          Diagram (b)

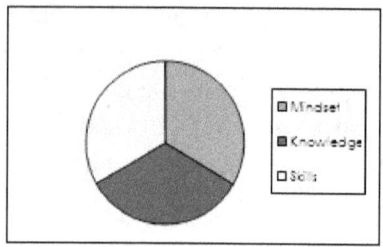
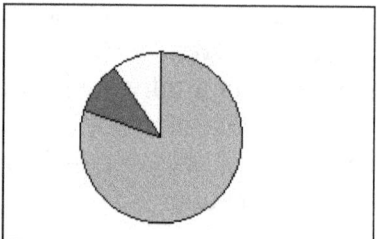

The irony is that if you ask the average Managing Director, HR Director or Training Manager how much time and effort is invested in training people to have the right mindset there will often be an uncomfortable silence.

In one conversation with a very successful rainmaker, who had built a practice from virtually nothing to dominate his adopted city, we enquired where he received his training in sales. The response was a puzzled *"What training? It needed to be done so we just got on with it."*

He did go on to lament the fact that many of the fee earners who had joined his firm after he had ploughed the way forward lacked the same level of drive and determination as he did. *"There are a bunch of young, highly paid solicitors who work here, I cannot understand why they don't have the same drive and they are just too complacent."* However he did realise that the use of a structured sales development programme would be valuable for the firm to help the junior partners accelerate their success.

It is clear that the professionals, if they haven't already done so, are waking up to the fact that to succeed they must learn how to make it rain. Being a technical specialist and brilliant at your job in today's market is not enough.

This experience immediately brought back a memory of a similar comment we'd heard some years before. In the late 90s and into the millennium we had the privilege to work with an 80-person change team in Rolls-Royce the multinational aerospace company. Their role was to persuade their colleagues to adopt modern procurement practices. The team was populated with technically expert purchasing professionals. During one workshop, called 'Persuading Powerful People,' we encountered the exact same issue. One participant yelled at the coach *"It's not my job to sell."*

This is one of the critical issues facing many professional services firms, that being a sense of identity. If these highly paid professionals do not believe that being a salesman is who they are, then no matter how much they are cajoled, pressurised and incentivised they will not adopt the attributes of a Rainmaker.

In one conversation one experienced lawyer told us that he struggled with the whole idea of selling. He was being asked to sell but no support was offered by the business apart from the odd 2-hour seminar on networking. Further discussion revealed a serious level of discomfort that, if left to fester, could have had long-term adverse consequences.

However the good news is that an experienced sales coach can address this interference and by equipping professionals with some simple strategies they can easily acquire the confidence to win substantial business.

Common sense suggests that some professionals are more cut out to sell than others. What is also clear and sometimes difficult for some fee earners to appreciate is that selling is far from being a dirty word. Selling can be boiled down to a series of simple and straightforward steps all of which are relatively easy to acquire as long as there is the burning desire and persistence to master them.

This revealed one of the many paradoxes in the professional services industry. Lawyers and accountants spend many years studying for their qualifications so they can practise. Firms ask their partners and fee earners to become Rainmakers yet comparatively little attention is given to training and educating people to sell. Selling itself is a profession which requires a high degree of skill and personal qualities all of which can easily be coached.

Firms are increasingly investing in training and coaching to provide a structured environment to develop and, in many cases, to keep their good people. Many of the larger firms have established academies or 'universities.' There is also evidence that there is a new breed of professionals coming out of the universities who have the confidence and will to sell themselves perhaps more so than the previous generation.

## 2.2 Am I doing what I am cut out to do?

A further example of mindset, two anecdotes that reveal an interesting conclusion:

In the late 90s we met a hugely successful lawyer at a book launch at Filbert Street, ex-home of Leicester City Football Club. The speaker, Adair Turner, ex-Director general of the CBI, inspired us to all think about where we were heading in our lives. Following the talk over a glass of wine the lawyer, who was obviously on a six-figure salary, lamented about how his success had opened doors leading to a senior-partner position in a local law firm. We asked him if where he was now matched his aspirations as a young man. He fell silent and answered *"no"*. We asked why and after careful thought he said that he had not made the big choices he wanted to make. His success had made them for him.

On another occasion we shared an intimate conversation with an accountant. A lovely guy who expressed sadness each time we spoke. He finally admitted that he didn't enjoy being an accountant at all.

The conclusion begs a question, how many professionals, once they qualify, limit their aspirations to their profession and is it healthy for them? The evidence, although difficult to quantify, suggests that professional service firms, in the main, are not particularly people-centred. In many firms there is an unhelpful attitude of *"you've done the training and are qualified, now just get on with it."* This is great for those who thrive in that environment and blatantly unhealthy for those that do not.

It is not the purpose of this document to persuade the reader to change their careers. Simply to suggest that it is not uncommon for people to 'wear a mask' at work which hides the incongruence between their career and their values and aspirations. This is a cause of deep dissatisfaction and, over the long term, potentially damaging.

## 2.3 Excuses, excuses, excuses!

A short and amusing story.

In the 90s we developed a training workshop entitled 'Breakthrough!' This was designed to help people recognise and eliminate any self imposed personal interference to success. During the programme we boldly and sombrely state that there exists within the majority of people a condition that affects the mind in the same way as cancer affects the body. It is called *'excusitis.'*

To illustrate this we brought a little fun and theatre to the workshop. A willing participant, who has been putting off doing something important, puts herself in the dock and on trial for not following through on a promise to herself.

The accused then tells everyone her excuses for not following through on her commitment and the remainder of the participants (the jury) pass their judgement on the validity of each excuse. This is great fun and it causes people to consider what excuses they make and what they genuinely have control and influence over.

These are some of the excuses revealed in this research. We shall leave you to consider whether they are valid or not.

**Diagram (c): Common excuses**

| Action required by the fee earner | Excuse |
|---|---|
| Spotting possible new business opportunities when engaged in a project within an account. | *"The time constraints and scope of the project do not allow me to find opportunities to ask peripheral questions that are unrelated to the project."* |
| Spending time educating people in the firm about what they do and learning about other parts of the business. | *"I haven't got the time."* <br> *"They don't want to learn."* |
| Taking time outside of normal working hours to attend marketing and business development activities e.g. networking events, award ceremonies, dinners etc. | *"This is violating my work vs home life balance."* |
| Learning and implementing new marketing and business development techniques and processes. | *"New regulations mean that the time I devote to learning is limited ensuring I am up to date with the changes brought in by new regulations. I don't have time to learn anything new that isn't directly related to the job I do."* |

| | "It's not my job." |
|---|---|
| Conducting research into how the customers perceive the quality of service delivered by the firm. | "I don't have time." "I don't know how to." |
| For the marketing department: Influencing the partners to apply science to their marketing activities. | "They just won't listen." |

## 2.4 I haven't got time to do marketing and selling

A classic and common excuse that merits exclusive attention.

During one interview with an equity partner we went through the 30 business development challenges and asked him what his top three challenges were. "Time to do it all" was the number one. In rather woeful tones he lamented about his target of 70% of time being fee earning and the rest caught up with managing the business.

Ironically we noticed that he had not set any time boundaries about when the interview would finish even though we had suggested 26 minutes on the phone. We normally do but on this occasion we had started the meeting 15 minutes late and we needed as much of his time as we could get. He was happy to talk for over an hour to us. We weren't sure whether he found our conversation particularly interesting, he was being particularly polite or he was not disciplined in his use of time. I suspect there was a large degree of the latter and a little denial in his excuse about not finding the time to engage in marketing and selling activities.

Naturally there is a balance to be found between work and home life. Many sales professionals 'make it' whilst retaining this balance. It is a question of establishing priorities and having the discipline to utilise proven time management techniques.

Appendix 4 reveals a set of proven time management disciplines.

## 2.5 Can you really teach an old dog new tricks?

Just about every respondent told us that there are two types of accountant/lawyer. The first is a technical specialist and the second a technical specialist that makes it rain. There was a shared, and in our opinion unhealthy, belief that once a person has demonstrated a reluctance to move out of their comfort zone and embrace new working practices that was it for life.

Is this true? Of course not. Our firm belief, as a firm of professional coaches, is that just about anyone can learn to do just about anything, it just takes some people a little longer to master a skill than others. All it requires is a vision of the future, burning desire, discipline and a                                    little                                    faith.

We had a delightful conversation with a very successful Architect who had run his own young business for 7 years. We asked him why he made the break. His response, *"I was never going to get to the next level with my Dad in charge of the firm I worked for. It was a training course that made the difference. The speaker literally inspired me to take life by the hands and make the decision to create my own future."*

It was plainly obvious that he enjoyed this life and could never go back. We also explored his views on service professionals. In the majority of cases he believed professionals i.e. doctors, lawyers, accountants and architects like doing what they are trained to do and selling is an unwanted yet necessary irritant.

However he had realised that the world had dramatically changed and that just being a professional was not enough. For example the look of his shop window was quite beautiful and awe-inspiring. He reminded me that in the old days solicitors had a bronze plaque next to the front door. Now in the local business park the name of the solicitors was emblazoned on the outside wall with 40 foot high letters! He said that if he had not moved with the times and embraced a modern approach to marketing and selling his business would not have survived.

Therein lays yet another paradox. People change because something somewhere lights the spark that says 'let's do it'. Yet there will always be a hankering to do what you are comfortable in doing. The difficulty many people face is that they live with the comfort of the known until the frustration of not changing becomes unbearable. For many this realisation comes too late and the consequence is deep regret.

We were delighted to hear from one marketing director about an in-house training and development programme delivering exceptional results. With great pride he related the story of one man who was on target to make partner at a relatively mature age of 59! This could only have been achieved through a co-ordinated and tailored series of development activities backed up by bags of support and encouragement

# 3: Are lawyers and accountants really that different from the rest of us?

This was one of the most frequently asked questions asked of us during the research. We heard many times that there are two types of professional, either 'the hunter and the grinder' or the 'rainmaker and the doer.' This part of the research looked into whether there are specific personality and behavioural traits amongst the professions and if they have a bearing on the ability to make it rain.

## 3.1 Studies of Rainmakers

Before we review the personality traits of lawyers and accountants we have highlighted the traits of successful salespeople irrespective of their profession.

Research reveals three traits:

The most important is **Ego Drive**, the desire to persuade others for the sheer sake of persuasion itself (and not necessarily because the person believes the underlying point that he or she is advocating). People with high Ego Drive love to persuade because when they get someone else to agree with them, it validates their identity or "Ego."

The second trait is **Empathy**. This is a desire to metaphorically step into the shoes of the other person to understand the world as seen through their eyes.

The third trait is **Resilience**, the ability to bounce back from criticism or rejection. When a prospect says "no", it just makes the sales person hungrier to try harder, whereas those with low resilience tend to take the rejection personally, feel rejected, and quickly lose their interest in selling.

As a business, we are loathe to pigeon-hole people as certain types as there is a risk that people begin to believe that they cannot change.

However it is right to suggest that the type of training lawyers and accountants receive has a significant bearing on their character and personality. It is therefore reasonable to suggest that people in these professions have certain personality and behavioural traits.

During our enquiries we found more research understanding the personality traits of lawyers than accountants. Consequently most of the following is targeted towards solicitors.

## 3.2 Personality traits of solicitors and accountants

Lawyers are trained to be rational and objective. This training, combined with the devaluation of emotional concerns and feelings, may cause them to perceive that a need for help from others is a character flaw. Due to their unique personality traits, lawyers may not recognise that they themselves may be the route of their own problems.

Lawyers also tend to have more 'masculine' traits. These include being argumentative, competitive, aggressive, and dominant. Consequently they may feel a sense of social isolation.

Lawyers in general have a low interest in emotional concerns and interpersonal matters and a disproportionate preference for thinking as opposed to feeling. They may prefer to spend more time dealing with information, the intellect, or interactions that emphasise the mind rather than the heart.

Generally lawyers work with a high sense of urgency. They may finish others' sentences, jump to conclusions, be impulsive and talk in clipped sentences. There is intensity to their behavioural style, since they are results-oriented. They seek efficiency and economy in everything from conversations to case management to relationships.

They can be perceived as brusque, poor listeners, and irritate many people. Meetings can be difficult and there may be a level of frustration and oppression in manager/direct report relationships.

There is an outward confidence and even boldness that characterises most lawyers although, as many of our clients and friends tell us, they are sensitive people under the surface. This is a reasonable cause to why so many partners' meetings get sidetracked into defensive exchanges and why a simple request to return a weekly report is often met with a defensive response.

A further trait amongst lawyers is a fierce need for autonomy. It is common for lawyers to resist being managed, to become indignant when being told what to do, and to prize their independence. As one senior partner lamented *"managing lawyers is like herding cats!"*

Lawyers are trained to be skeptical, judgmental, questioning and argumentative. This may be perceived by others as cynical and self-protective. In much of the work carried out by lawyers e.g. litigation, tax or mergers and acquisitions these traits are valuable. However if there is an inability to switch off the skepticism then this becomes an unhelpful trait especially when it comes to forming relationships, selling and behaving appropriately in meetings.

Accountants have excellent organisational skills and extraordinary powers of concentration to create order and structure in their lives. They have strong opinions about the way things should be done. They value tradition, security, stability, and are practical and down-to-earth.

They will work long and hard to fulfil duties and can be depended on to follow through on tasks. Accountants are generally precise, detail-oriented, analytical and neat. Many perceive them as quiet, less aggressive, more studious, less spontaneous and risk averse.

The conclusion. The answer to the question *'Are lawyers and accountants any different from the rest of us?'* is yes. In general terms accountants and lawyers are likely to have certain personality traits. Some of which will be conducive to rainmaking and others will be counterproductive.

However, it is important to be very careful when labeling people. If you catch someone saying that *"All lawyers/accountants are..."* then remind them that they are likely to have insecurities, fears, traits, habits, values and beliefs just like everyone else.

## 3.3 To what degree does ego inhibit success?

Some of the financial advisors we interviewed and have worked with over the years are under no illusion that the majority of solicitors and accountants are egotistical, narrow-minded, ultra protective, in self denial about how talented they really are and unbelievably difficult to deal with. Ask a solicitor or an accountant the same question and of course you'll hear a different story!

We learned of an extremely talented accountant who had a huge number of staff working for him in his own practice. Unfortunately the firm had not moved on for the best part of a decade. His profits were consistently minimal despite an impressive turnover and it was clear he was overstaffed. Although he struggled to admit it he didn't enjoy managing his team. We also found out that his team didn't respect his leadership (but the pay was good!).

A close friend asked him why he carried on this way working extremely hard, doing long hours, carrying out tasks he neither enjoyed or was particularly good at, whilst upsetting and unsettling the majority of his staff all for minimal return? Why didn't he just work with a PA and spend the majority of his time doing what he excelled at?

There was only one answer. His ego. It would not allow him to face the facts of his reality and allow him to consider options. Bizarre!

During the research, in some of the interviews, we asked the question, *"Are professionals in your firm arrogant and do they display patronising behaviour?"* The answer of course is that some do and some don't. For many their total focus is on the technical aspects of their job, they enjoy it, work hard it and feel extremely comfortable with what they do.

The people side is not considered important and they don't know any other way. The projection to others however, whilst often unintentional, can often be perceived as humourless, non-responsive and arrogant. We were not surprised to learn that those that did display this behaviour rarely, if ever, received any feedback on the consequences of their actions and what they would have to do to improve. C'est la vie.

By the way one of our closest associates is a company accountant. He is bright, brilliant with people and one of the funniest people we know!

## 3.4 Is being right persuasive?

Three stories, one personal and two professional which illustrate a point.

Someone who we know intimately is a hugely intelligent, powerful and successful entrepreneur. He works hard at everything and has, by his own admission, only one significant fault, his massive ego. It is very difficult for him to accept that he isn't right. More times than not he is and can back up his point of view with well-researched reasoned arguments. However when it comes to persuading people of his view it becomes incredibly irritating when your argument is countered by an even bigger one. At the end of the conversation with him you feel as though your mind has just gone through ten rounds with Mike Tyson!

Recently we worked with a sales team in a leading training and coaching company. We noticed that the top sales exec, who consistently out-performed her peers by a significant margin, had some serious challenges connecting with her colleagues. During a feedback session, where we were invited to give constructive feedback to each other we asked if she used the same behaviours when persuading her colleagues as she did when face-to-face with a customer.

After a short pause she caught on to the point of the question and suggested otherwise. With customers she listened intently, with colleagues she led with reasoned arguments which were repeated and became louder in the face of resistance.

We were invited by the sales director to coach her and over time she found herself becoming far more successful in persuading her colleagues when she treated them in the same way as her customers.

In the late 90s I had the privilege to work with a team of technically proficient specialists in Rolls-Royce Aerospace. They were charged with delivering a significant change into the business which meant persuading their colleagues in the line to adopt new working practices.

After eighteen months of immense effort they were struggling to deliver the changes that the business demanded. On closer examination it became obvious that their lack of success was due to the fact that their approach largely consisted of making logical compelling arguments for change. Their 'push style' persuasion was predominantly *"do this for these reasons and it will be good for you"*.

Their lives changed considerably when we coached them to adopt a consultative 'pull style' approach. This begins with giving the customer a 'damn good listening to' uncovering the issues followed by a carefully constructed solution that matches the expressed needs of the customer.

The following diagram (a) reveals a significant shift in the way products and services are sold in the 21$^{st}$ Century vs 20$^{th}$ Century. Increasing emphasis is on building rapport and relationships.

**Diagram (d)**

**20th vs 21st Century selling**

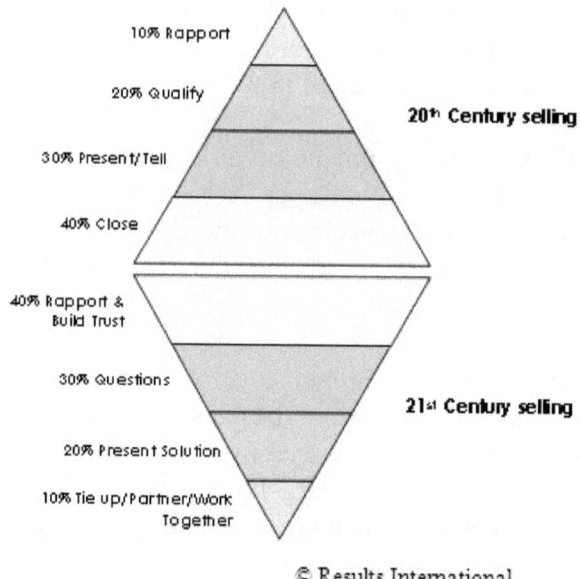

10% Rapport

20% Qualify

30% Present/Tell

40% Close

**20th Century selling**

40% Rapport & Build Trust

30% Questions

20% Present Solution

10% Tie up/Partner/Work Together

**21st Century selling**

© Results International

One partner told us that *'one of the difficulties of working with lawyers is that we're trained to be right.'* This is great when you are trying to win a contentious case. However in normal conversation it often limits the ability to listen.

# 4: Corporate Culture

Culture is defined as the norms that define how society behaves. Corporate culture has a significant bearing on business success; and it is a function of many things including branding, symbols, organisation structure, systems, policies, heritage and leadership. In our own history as a business, in the UK and around the world, we have experienced every type of culture from the free thinking and adventurous to the suspicious and fearful; outrageous and fun to the boring and rigid; dynamic and forward thinking to the indifferent and predictable.

We were curious to find out if there was a generic culture in professional services firms or if there were significant differences between our respondents.

We concluded that there are significant differences in culture between firms and even offices. Five of the businesses we contacted chose not to participate; one partner said about his firm *'we are paranoid about secrecy'* they simply would not let us have the name of the marketing director. Only first names were given. What's that all about? We felt as though we were talking to the thought police from a 1960's firm in Eastern Europe. I cannot imagine how that environment could foster the creativity, innovation and risk taking essential in any sales driven environment.

Cheekily, we still wanted to learn what the business was doing so, faced with this objection, we contacted one of the partners in the regions. He was more than happy to tell us about the firm and agreed that there were people in HQ who weren't exactly in tune with the reality of the front line.

## 4.1 Does success require you be macho?

We completed a piece of research with a hugely successful practice and were invited to share our findings with the senior partner who was also a Master Rainmaker. We told him that there were instances where some of the partners felt disenfranchised from the inner sanctums of power in the business.

We told him that during a one-to-one conversation with one of the junior partners, he had told us, in confidence, that he was lonely. Whilst this was the exception, the senior partner's response was mildly alarming. He suggested that people who had this attitude and displayed this behaviour were 'wimps.'

After a little more dialogue he reluctantly suggested that this was an unhealthy label to give anyone. We did remind him that he had hired this 'wimp' in the first place!

Another senior partner lamented at length that his team's hunger was diminishing. It was quite astonishing to see the look of anguish on his face as he described how his junior colleagues would complain about their 'quality of life violations.' He did go on to reveal that being married to his work had had many negative consequences in his own life.

Many of the women we spoke to complain bitterly about the ego, posturing and old boys network in their firms.

This indicates that in many firms there is a male 'type A' dominated macho culture. Of course there is everything right with being driven, competitive, successful, hard-working and goal-oriented. However in all our experience we have yet to find any successful professional who has not gone through periods of self-doubt, confusion, unease, frustration and fear. Whilst, professionally, most will hide these periods from their colleagues unless there is a strong support network a sustained period 'in the wilderness', can be damaging. Unfortunately others will only see a dip in performance and behaviour which they deem inappropriate. They may draw unhealthy judgments about the individual which serves only to compound the problem.

Ironically we also discovered in one firm if they knew one of their valued clients was suffering from a serious personal issue they would lavish them with attention. The prevalent attitude in the firm seemed to be: 'empathise with the customer and support them at all costs but admonish any of our own people who exhibit weakness.' Another interesting paradox.

## 4.2 Leadership is everything

Undoubtedly leadership style has a significant impact upon an organisation's culture and culture has a significant impact on the commitment people have to their employer and therefore to sales success. During one research project we had the opportunity to interview a cross section of the partners.

We reached the conclusion that we would not be able to help them deliver the step change in sales performance unless there was a significant, sustainable and positive shift in the attitude and behaviour of some of the senior partners.

However when we enquired whether there was anything in place to help the partners learn how to manage people, there was no response. This situation is not unlike many industries in the UK where leaders are given a management position on account of their technical skill and track record. Yet when they get into a position where they manage people they are given little guidance. It is no wonder that one senior solicitor told us *"To be honest I'd rather not manage people; I'd just like to carry on with what I am trained to do."*

We suspect there are many that share this sentiment. Creating inspirational leaders is one, if not the greatest, challenge organisations face.

## 4.3 Do professional services firms need empowered people?

One ex-lawyer and current senior Head of People Development in a top 10 accountancy told us *"I wanted a new challenge and decided to move from law to accountancy. I had many offers and I chose my current employer because of the vibrant and progressive culture."*

One partner told us that his company had radically changed in the last 6 years and become totally values-driven. He could never see it going back to the old ways.

Customer feedback is a critical issue but corporate culture is the 'biggy'. Businesses should empower and involve staff, ensure the people at the top embody the brand values, and be prepared to embrace the changes that consumers dictate. Nurturing a customer-centric view of operating such as this means much more than simply having written down processes and scripts to cover every eventuality.

The senior movers and shakers need to notice what it is that they do that works. They need to find out in what ways their beliefs and behaviours make their business flourish so they can do more of what matters. Employees can also play an active role. It could be that some of the organisation's success flows from the way staff are treated, who in turn treat customers well. Anyone who has made a decision about a restaurant based on the way a waiter responds, will appreciate how pivotal this interaction can be. It therefore pays to be responsive to a workforce's opinions and ideas.

Some years ago we conducted a study of the correlation between employee satisfaction and customer satisfaction across six similar businesses. Interestingly and unsurprisingly the results were conclusive. Simply the businesses that had satisfied employees, who felt 'connected' to the business and empowered to make change happen, had satisfied customers (and they were more profitable over the long term).

## 4.4 Are the partners motivated to align themselves and work effectively with their colleagues?

The majority of firms were organised into separate businesses with a focus on subject matter, industry sector and geography. Many cited their success because of their niche. This was regarded as essential to foster autonomy, entrepreneurial flair and expertise in specific areas.

The downside was the creation of a silo mentality. Many partners were seen as over protective of their clients, unwilling to actively share their experience and hesitant in adopting common sales practices.

In one interview we spent 30 minutes deciding why professionals might be behaving this way. It came down to a simple equation: What's in it for me (WIIFM) v What's against my interest (WAMI). See diagram (e). If the WAMI is greater than the WIIFM then there is an absence of the required behaviour.

In essence there is no reason why partners should not involve other people. However it may require a change in the structure and reward systems to drive the changes in behaviour. One city accountancy had set itself up in a matrix structure to encourage the partners to freely and openly co-operate to exploit opportunities in specific market sectors and clients.

**Diagram (e)**

**Forces for and against sharing client information and sales opportunities with colleagues.**

| What's against my interest? | What's in it for me? |
| --- | --- |
| • Negative impact on my ability to achieve my targets<br>• I don't know enough about other people's capabilities<br>• I don't trust my colleagues<br>• I don't like my colleagues<br>• I've achieved a lot without anyone's help so why involve anyone else?<br>• They might reveal my weaknesses<br>• The client might prefer them | • It demonstrates professionalism and our full capability when experts are introduced to the client<br>• The extra pair of eyes may spot an opportunity I have overlooked<br>• We can learn to work together and build a trusting relationship that will bear fruit in the future<br>• My colleagues and I will grow as a result of working together<br>• My colleagues will reciprocate with their own personal |

| | |
|---|---|
| to me<br>• It will take too long to educate them | introductions<br>• I will learn more about the business<br>• It will help me to learn how to coach more effectively<br>• More business! |

## 4.5 The impact of being part of a recognised and traditional profession

During one conversation with a solicitor and long-time friend he mourned the demise of law as a profession and how, in the eyes of others including friends and family, the prestige surrounding the title lawyer or solicitor had diminished. He spoke of the effort he had put in over many years to qualify and train and how frustrated and upset he was at the lack of recognition he and his colleagues felt. When we explored the reasons further he cited highly publicised malpractice and the law society as the primary culprit.

We did wonder why he was spending so much thinking time worrying about issues over which he had minimal influence or control.

We wondered about the impact of this belief and how this state of denial and blame was hindering his progress. When we enquired about what active marketing he was doing it sadly became clear that he was not fully embracing reality and consequently doing very little to address the harsh commercial realities of a very competitive world.

We suspect this is a prevalent belief amongst many of his peers especially the smaller operators.

## 4.6 Punching above your weight, why living your values helps you beat the competition

"We beat Shoosmiths to win an award... we wrestled an account away from Eversheds."

Two comments from a business development executive who demonstrated how unshakable self-belief, attachment to brand values, hard work and commitment was taking her relatively small business into new, exciting and extremely profitable territory.

Have you ever come across these values in business?

- Friendly and approachable
- Easy to do business with
- Straight talking
- Speak and write in crystal clear English
- Pragmatic
- Roll your sleeves up and get the job done
- Working in partnership, 'shoulder to shoulder' with the client

This set of values were developed by her firm. They were the result of an extensive 360 degree study of how they perceived themselves and how they were perceived by their customers, associates and partners.

It was clear that a huge level of energy and commitment was being paid to both discovering the values and making sure all the staff lived and breathed them. She took great delight by telling us that she enjoyed hearing about how some of the larger firms were spending huge sums of money on re-branding without consistently putting the effort in to driving the changes in behaviour of the fee earners throughout the organisation.

Her firm was winning business from the larger competitors on the strength that they were, in the eyes of the customer, congruent i.e. consistently behaving in a manner that matched their stated values.

One example she delighted in telling us was how her previous employer, a large law firm, hired (in her exact words) a *pompous, arrogant and aggressive Oxford graduate.'* Apparently he made sure that the customer knew that he knew everything. He told them that he would help them *'beat up the competition.'* Yet the brand values said that his firm would listen, partner and seek win-win solutions! Maybe the firm should be more honest and put together some different values.

We had some fun putting together some alternatives:

*"Bludgeon Solicitors. Instruct us and:*

- *We'll tell you what to do.*
- *We'll make sure you are impressed by how clever we think we really are.*
- *We'll beat the BLEEP! out of anyone who dares to cross you or us.*
- *We'll crow about ourselves and patronise you at every possible opportunity.*
- *We'll talk and write in a way that makes us feel amazingly clever and important.*
- *When you feel rather thick and inferior and at your weakest point we'll give you a massive bill.*
- *We'll charge you a shed load of money for stuff we know and don't think you need to know or couldn't possibly comprehend because we are much smarter than you.*
- *We'll smile in your presence and make uncomplimentary comments about you behind your back. "*

Maybe there is a customer out there that wants this?

In summary, brand values are vital and worth taking the time to uncover and gain consensus. We know one company that spent two years working with all its 130,000 staff across the world to gain agreement to their values.
The key is getting everyone to consistently live and breathe them. This means people have to change their beliefs, attitude and behaviour. Now that is a challenge!

# 5: Organisation and speed of change

In one interview with a business development executive from a top 5 2nd tier accountancy practice we were told in unequivocal terms *"partnerships are different, it takes ages for change to happen around here."* We spent a little while quizzing the respondent what he meant by this.

He responded with quips as reasons for inertia: *"management by committee"*, *"the largest and loudest egos get their way"*, *"hidden sanctums of power"*, *"everyone wanting a say in the decision"*.

We concluded that a carefully orchestrated approach for bringing about change works in any organisation, it's just a question of being smart about the way you do it.

We asked him how he gets the decision makers in his larger clients to align themselves around a proposed solution. He talked about doing the initial research to find out where the pain exists and its impact on the business; developing a compelling argument for change; persuading the advocates to buy into him, his firm and the proposed solution; carefully structuring presentations and meetings to bring other people on board; gaining consensus and finally going for the close.

After getting the yes and closing the business he said they carefully delivered the solution with detailed programme management to leave the customer delighted with the outcome. Here's the kicker, we asked him if he and his colleagues applied the same rigour to bringing in changes within his own firm. The deafening silence implied another paradox!

The conclusion is that bringing about change in any organisation is simply a question of finding the right approach. Over the past decade we have discovered the 10-steps that organisations go through, irrespective of the nature of the change, the size of the population affected by the change or the market sector. Details of the steps are given in appendix 5.

# 6: Communication

"I didn't know that!" is a common complaint with Rainmakers.

No surprises here, few companies in the world have got communication absolutely right. One marketing director suggested that in some cases poor communication had caused him to write off billing time through a lack of co-ordination between the fee earners working on an account. A tough decision had to be made to protect the firm's reputation even though there was a significant loss of profit.

Communication has a significant impact on culture. In one of our clients we came across a leader who was fond of delivering monthly stump speeches and surprise announcements to 'rally the troops.'
The trouble was he was so bad at it, it had the opposite effect. The managers present had to re-deliver the same speech once they returned to their office whilst apologising profusely for the behaviour of their leader!

Research reveals seven ingredients all of which are necessary for ensuring communications work in your firm:

1. Expect that people will need to hear the same message at least three times in three different ways before they understand it.
2. Use every medium possible to introduce and reinforce key messages. Always spoken first, written second.
3. Use this well-known mantra.
   - Tell me I forget
   - Show me I remember
   - Involve me I understand
4. Regularly ask for feedback from your team on how well you are communicating and act on it!
5. Regularly refresh the methods with which you communicate.
6. Leaders should learn to communicate well or empower an effective communicator to deliver the message.
7. If you want to involve people become a brilliant facilitator.

Incidentally there is only one company we know of where employees have actually stated that the company communicated too well!

# 7: Reward and recognition

The purpose of this line of enquiry was to understand if any pay systems had a significant impact. The research was inconclusive. Some believed that their systems prompted protectionist, empire building behaviour, others did not.

Some businesses have moved away from individual bonuses to one single profit pot shared on a firm-wide basis. This has caused the fee earners to consider what is best for the firm and not themselves.

Some firms rewarded their people on financial performance as well as adherence to the firms values. This is in line with leading edge thinking across the business world. More than one firm is moving to a position where the partners are rewarded on more than just what fees they bring to the business. Other factors including technical capability, commercial acumen, teamwork, relationship building, customer retention and customer satisfaction were included.

Jack Welch, the ex CEO of General Electric, created a model (c). His view is simple, if you evaluate and reward people on the extent to which they live the businesses values it will promote the behaviours you want.

# Diagram (f) The Jack Welch Model

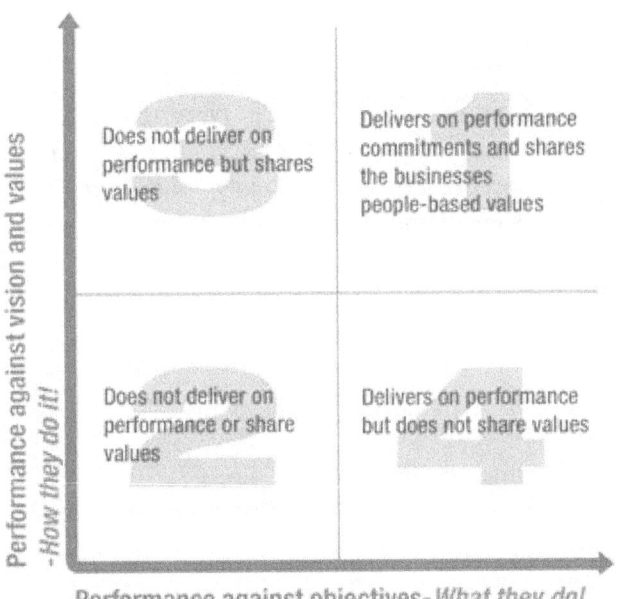

Quite simply he says getting people to quadrant 1 is always the goal. Quadrant 2 is easy, fire them! People in quadrant 3 require patience, support and coaching. Quadrant 4 is always the problem. Jack Welsh is unequivocal. People here will eventually cause more harm than good, retain people in quadrant 4 at your peril!

Interestingly and coincidently one of our clients has recognised that without going through this process of gaining consensus around their vision and values they will not be able to take the business to the next level.

A leading accounting firm told us that one of the behaviours they wanted to see more of were the fee earners exchanging more Personal Introductions (PIs) or referrals. They simply put a pot of money aside and anyone who passes on a PI that translated into business would receive a small percentage of the fees.

A final word on recognition, we could find little evidence of firms giving public recognition for sales success. In one firm a specialist team had secured a major contract from right under the nose of the much larger competitor. Despite the enormity of the achievement nobody knew about it other than a footnote on a page on the intranet that nobody ever looked at!

In our experience many firms specialise in passing on bad news. The successful ones consciously reverse this. They work hard at countering the grapevine by continuously pumping out positive messages through many and varied media and communications channels.

# 8: Managing people

## 8.1 Do I know what I'm doing?

Just occasionally when we are engaged in a research project we hear something that makes us giggle. We were engaged in an in-depth chat with an ex-KPMG partner who is making his mark specialising in corporate finance. He talked about the importance of relationship building and patience. Some of his mega-deals were taking 2 years to close.

The conversation drifted into talking about his colleagues and suddenly he looked at us with an exasperated face commenting:

*"Some of our people are prone to not thinking about what they are doing!"* He went on *"Selling is relatively straightforward, so many people choose the hard route when there is so much low hanging fruit around."*

Unfortunately the best efforts of the management team were not causing them to change their approach.

It reminded us of the classic observation that everyone involved in training and coaching appreciates. Often it is the case that people that take coaching and training seriously are normally the ones that need it least!

The question is: *'How do you get people to want to change their approach and adopt new habits when the ones they have now are not delivering the results the business needs?'* There is only one answer: feedback.

## 8.2 How am I doing?

*"Feedback is the breakfast of champions."* is a famous phrase coined by Ken Blanchard in his best-selling book 'The one minute manager' many years ago.

On the way up in law firms and accountancy practices feedback is given frequently. However, once people reach the top, in the majority of cases, the feedback tap is switched off.

One practice leader said that, apart from the end-of-year review, there were no formal or even informal mechanisms for letting people know how they are doing. In another practice one partner lamented *"Around here you are left alone as long as you are delivering the numbers. When you aren't they give you lots of feedback although I wouldn't necessarily call it that."*
He did go on to say that he did deliver the numbers but felt quite lonely. It was clear he wanted to be reminded that he was doing things well.

One situation that made us smile was a senior partner who stated that he managed to improve the performance of a junior partner considerably just by getting him to stop wearing brown shoes. A trip to the tailor plus some coaching from the female members of the team apparently did the trick. He did go on to say that the guy with body odour was a tougher nut to crack!

Research across many business sectors reveals a progression in the level and quality of feedback. The ultimate destination is what we call 'Dynamic 360.' This is where everyone in the business is active in regularly seeking and acting on feedback from multiple sources – the boss, peers, direct reports, customers, suppliers and partners.

Diagram (d) illustrates feedback progression from the straightforward top down annual appraisal through to Dynamic 360 where people are openly and constantly seeking and acting on feedback from multiple sources.

## Diagram (g)

### Dynamic 360 - the evolution of feedback

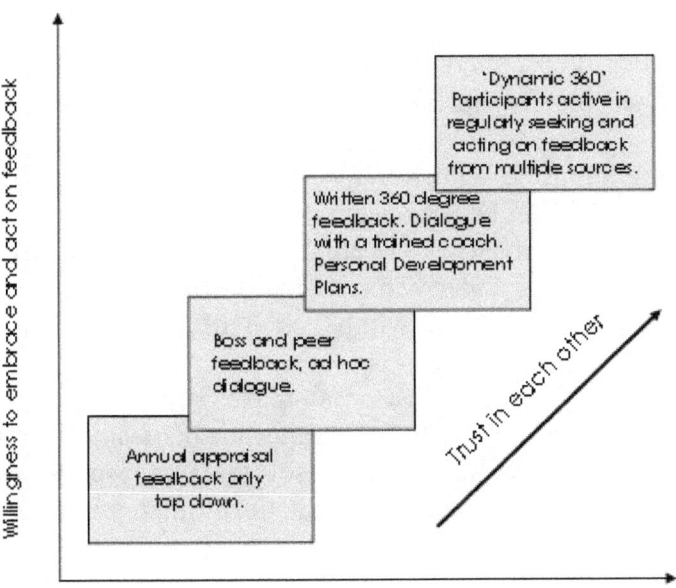

Frequency and richness of feedback

## 8.3 I don't want to be measured on how well I'm doing

There is a timeless adage in business *'what gets measured gets done.'* It seems that apart from billable hours there are few other meaningful and consistently used business development measures in law and accounting firms. A great lesson learned many years ago from a good friend in financial services is the power of keeping a record of personal activity and sales achievement. He went from a standing start of 0 to 600 customers in just 6 years and is enjoying the considerable fruits of his labours today.

He regularly measures the following:

- Percentage of retained business
- Volume of new business
- Number of business meetings

- Average number of business meetings required with a client to close the business
- Outcomes from each business meeting
- Conversion ratios
- Return per client (his goal is to focus his time only on the 20% of customers who deliver 80% of the revenue)
- Customer satisfaction

The key is the rigour he applied to measurement. If this is the key to success then why doesn't everyone do it?

The answer: because most people are scared of what they will find out about themselves and by measuring themselves there is an implication that massive action will be required!

We discussed this with one Master Rainmaker and he told us that it would be too difficult and time consuming for his team to measure their activity and achievement along these lines. Our response was to ask him how serious he was about dramatically increasing personal performance.


## 8.4 Our meetings are a waste of time

Our personal pet subject! We have an absolute obsession with meetings having experienced more than our fair share of disasters that waste everyone's time.

Observing meetings is a good barometer to gauge how well a business is led. Anything from formal partners' meetings to ad hoc impromptu corridor meetings provide a terrific indication of how efficiently time and energy is spent when people get together.

During one research study we asked a selection of fee earners how they rated the quality of meetings in the firm. On a scale of 1 to 10 where 10 was outstanding the average score was 4. Further investigation revealed the common faults with the meetings. Here are just a few:

- Participants turning up late or not at all
- Little preparation
- Lack of clear purpose
- Poorly constructed agenda
- Discussions that wander off the subject
- An unskilled chair and or a skilled chair who chooses not to deploy her skills
- Poor environment

We're sure you know many more. Our belief is that most people actually know how to run meetings yet choose not to consistently do what they know is right. Yet another paradox is that when the fee earners were asked how well they ran meetings with customers the rating shot up. Bizarre!

A list of tips for preparing to lead meetings both internally and with customers, is given in appendix 6.

# 9: The role of marketing

On this subject opinions varied widely. For example one firm we interviewed employed a non-fee earning equity partner who enjoyed huge respect, credibility and influence. In this case all the production of marketing literature and PR is outsourced and a small team of highly paid and professional marketing professionals wield significant power in the firm. He told us that no tenders would be submitted before passing his desk.

Another city accounting practice had hired an impressive team of marketing professionals with the express goal to add an additional 24% return to their already impressive growth.

One lawyer told me that he wanted the business to employ a door opener. Someone who would do all the networking and hand him the business as he was simply not interested in selling himself.

On the other hand, one marketing representative of one of the big four complained at length how difficult it was to get air time with the partners who did their own thing with little or no reference to the marketing specialists. He mentioned that they had conducted an internal survey and no one could actually agree a definition for marketing and what they thought the role of the marketing specialists should be!

This is one of the key challenges faced by people in non-line roles to win the hearts and minds of the fee earners.

Most disagreed that there was an opportunity for a professional services firm to 'blow the competition away.' (We suspect they held this belief because their firms weren't doing so!)
However more than one respondent, with strong marketing pedigrees, agreed that any firm could do for law and accountancy what Larry Ellison has done for Oracle and in doing so they would make a mint.

A business development executive from a regional branch of a top ten accountancy firm told us how proud he was to work for a business that *'didn't behave like a traditional accountancy practice.'* He mentioned an impressive growth record from £6m to £15m achieved in a very short time by a small team of talented and sales-focused professionals.

The simple conclusion is that firms must become increasingly sales and marketing led and credible heavyweights must take the lead.

# 10: Selling professional services

It may seem a little strange that a report entitled 'Making it Rain' has a chapter on selling at number 10. We hope by now there is an appreciation that there is much to consider to when create an environment where Rainmakers can flourish and grow.

## 10.1 Working together and keeping the sales antennae switched on

During one study it became clear that there was an extensive 'silo mentality' in the firm. Only a select few at the top of the business were fully aware of the full capability of the business. These leaders were encouraging all the fee earners to get out and about and sell. The issue was that they could not spot the opportunities due to their lack of understanding of the firm's total service capability. We liken this to the person who buys a new car, (which is significantly different from one they have driven before), once they start looking for the new car they spot them everywhere!

The same principle applies to not understanding the full capability of your firm. If the fee earners do not understand, how can they possibly spot the opportunities put in front of them?

Larger firms must invest more time and energy in cross-department communication. A simple first step is simply conducting presentations to inform each other of what they do, why they do it and how they do it plus what a good potential client looks and sounds like!

Another step is to set up processes to swap personal introductions with colleagues. There are numerous networking organisations throughout the UK. In the larger firms it would be relatively easy to adopt similar processes internally. Done well these can be both productive and fun.

In one firm it was clear that some partners were holding back from introducing their colleagues into their existing clients as the following illustration (d) demonstrates. In this example the corporate solicitors had strong relationships with their clients and would not allow the employment law team access. This was causing frustration and even resentment within the firm since it was clear to the employment law team that there were significant opportunities to be exploited.

**Diagram (h)**

**Flow of information and communication within a law firm**

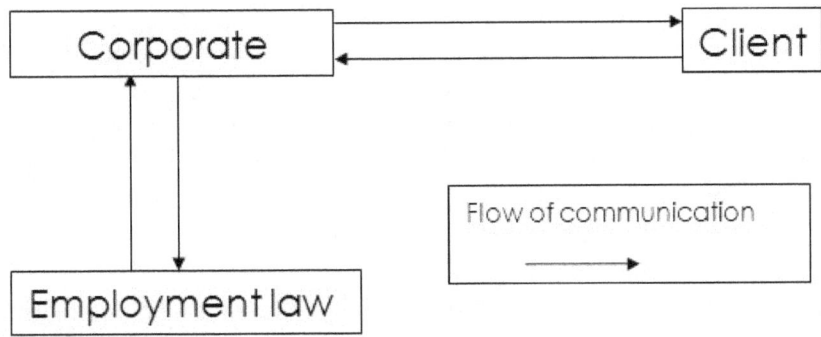

Another important step is to develop an account management methodology in the firm. Businesses who are smart at working together to win new business, and/or exploit further sales opportunities in accounts, adopt a common account management language. This ensures that when people come together from different parts of the business to form account or campaign teams they work together effectively.

Our extensive research working with Rain Makers across numerous market sectors has revealed **'The 7 behaviours of high performing account managers.'** See appendix 7.


## 10.2 Wowing the customer in a beauty parade

On several occasions we enquired about how partners won business in a competitive tendering situation and whether they did anything that put them ahead of the competition. It is clear that this is a key skill for fee earners to acquire both in giving powerful presentations, writing persuasive proposals and crucially doing the right amount of preparation.

Some firms are even hiring professional marketers and business development specialists to assist with the tender process. The investment in time and money to deliver an excellent pitch rises with the pressure to gain a good return on the investment.

One hugely successful Rainmaker, who delighted in regularly 'out-pitching' her rivals, told me that preparation was everything. Her extensive network allowed her to find out personal details about each of the decision makers. She would also enter the room with an impressive set of full ring binders chock full of research supporting the proposal. Her clients regularly tell her that the reason they enjoy working with her is because of her attention to detail, her individuality and her calm yet focused approach.

Another Rainmaker said that they kept on beating the opposition without the use of PowerPoint. Hurrah!

Another told us they won the business because the bid team simply sat and had coffee with the decision makers. This informal style was in keeping with the client's approach to business.

One other Rainmaker told us of their secret weapon. A lady in his office is a leading light in the local amateur dramatic scene. Before they deliver a presentation at a beauty parade they always rehearse the pitch before her. I was advised that anyone caught scratching or fiddling with themselves was severely reprimanded!

The conclusion, the key ingredients to delivering a presentation in a beauty parade that wows the customer are:

- Attention to detail in the research

- Gaining access and learning from the decision makers and key influencers prior to the pitch
- Finding out about the people who will be making the decision and flexing the approach to suit their values
- Delivering a solution that matches what they say they need and not what you think they should have
- Doing something different to grab the attention of the customer and disorientate their expectations
- Putting people in front of the customer who can relate to the personalities of the audience
- Being choosy about what to pitch for and what not to pitch for

## 10.3   So how do we let the customer know we are different from everyone else?

In an extremely competitive world it is crucial that professional service firms have the ability to let the customer know why they are different from anyone else.

The research revealed five main ways that firms are differentiating themselves.

Firstly, it is stating the obvious to say that every professional practice is different as it relies on people. The quality of the relationship with the client is what makes the difference. An example of this is one respondent who told us that a recent survey of customers indicated that they enjoyed doing business with his firm because the solicitors were so individual. His challenge was how to retain that differentiator whilst maintaining a consistent style and approach across the firm.

Second is unparalleled service. Those fee earners who demand the highest standards from themselves and their colleagues who work with the customer are the ones who consistently succeed. Standards of dress, speech, written word, response times, doing what you say you are going to do etc are all critical.

Third, and arguably the most important, is doing a great job. One lawyer told me the reason she was so successful was that she always won her cases. This fostered positive-word-of-mouth-advertising.

Fourth is having a niche. We know a number of very successful firms that have decided to become specialist lawyers or accountants in a specific sector. One local firm only works with individuals who have at least a £1 million income, another only works with Asian businesses, another with the IT sector. Having a niche means you can take the time to understand your sector and focus your marketing/networking resources.

Fifth, and the most intriguing, is doing something out of the ordinary. This makes talking about what your firm does more interesting.

One marketing director of an accounting firm told us that they were delivering training courses to the police on cyber–fraud. They had even involved the FBI in the course development and delivery!

Now imagine if you were at a party and you met two new people. You politely enquire *"so what do you do"* Their responses are:

Person (a)
"I'm an accountant, we do business recovery, audits and tax"

Person (b)
"We are in the money business, a recent example of what we do is train the fraud squad to use the internet to combat crime, and at the same time coach our clients to save money by understanding the complexities of accounting."

Who would you rather speak to?

**10.4 Networking**

A mid-size law firm reported that the partners had begun to realise that the traditional dinners, networking events, lunches, award ceremonies etc were becoming less effective in terms of return on the considerable investment in time and expense. However networking activities were considered important for developing the brand even though direct results were not always achieved.

In this case the marketing department were starting to have an impact by asking some detailed questions that caused the fee earners to revisit their traditional marketing methods. For example the partners were encouraged to set objectives prior to attending an event and then reporting back to the senior partner.

One partner lamented. *"I have dozens of business cards from all these events and do nothing with them."*

The research revealed that it was more useful to target specific individuals with innovative marketing and networking techniques rather than adopting a scatter gun *'I hope I bump into somebody important today'* approach.

In the original research we made a statement that the most effective form of advertising is through personal introductions or PIs (otherwise known as referrals).

All the respondents said that they needed to improve their ability to generate more and better personal introductions.

One marketing director said that the partners were just beginning to ask their valued clients questions 'who else do you know who…' He said that previously many were just too embarrassed to ask the question. They felt it too intrusive.

One Master Rainmaker remarked *"I go to hundreds of lunches, dinners and social events and quite frankly I get extremely bored with the same old conversations. However I have to keep alert as you never know when an opportunity will be discussed that I can latch onto."* Many of the Master Rainmakers tell us that the ability to generate personal introductions from the people they come into contact with is a key ingredient of their success.

**10.5 Is it really possible to energise everyone in the business to sell?**

Many of the firms we work with have asked us to look at ways in which they can galvanise the hearts and minds of the workforce so that they are motivated to look for opportunities to sell. As one partner commented; *"How am I going to motivate a 48 year old compliance-administrator who's been here for 30 years and never sold a thing to promote this business?"*

The research revealed 7 strategies a business can adopt that, when used simultaneously, will create the environment where people are motivated to sell.

- Help them develop the mindset that creates a belief that they can and want to sell.
- Train everyone in the business to look for opportunities that match the services the firm offers.
- Train and coach people so they naturally attract customers.
- Measure people on their sales activity and achievement.
- Ensure people know what's in it for them by celebrating, communicating and rewarding success.
- Make the whole process fun and exciting.

Have patience and stick at it!

# 11: Deliver exceptional service

It will not have gone unnoticed to the majority of business professionals that the boundaries between sales and service are blurring at an increasing rate. Firms are looking at service as one of their primary differentiators; speed of response, attention to detail, undivided attention to the customer, flexibility of doing businesses as well as relationships are all potential weapons to use against the competition.

## 11.1 Is it important to invest time measuring quality and service?

The answer is an unequivocal yes, however out of all the businesses interviewed none said they had sufficient multiple, rigorous and systematic processes for measuring the quality of service they provide. Many could not see the need for it. Some recognised the need but felt it was too low a priority. Some were enlisting the help of external agencies to solicit customer feedback and a few were looking to base a proportion of their remuneration on metrics based on feedback from customers.

The concept of customer loyalty is one of the accepted cornerstones of modern marketing. However, the last couple of decades has seen a relentless increase in the power of the client. They know their rights, feel confident about complaining and have high expectations of the products and services they buy. This independence means that clients cannot be assumed to be passive recipients of brands; instead customers actively decide where and what they will consume and if they don't get what they want they have no compunction about going elsewhere. The knock-on effect is that 'customer loyalty' has become a redundant concept. This begs two important questions:

If loyalty is a thing of the past, then how can firms hope to retain their clients?
What techniques and behaviours do they have to develop in order to make sure they stay on-side?

Even in accounting where, traditionally, customer loyalty extends to years customers are looking for more. Not just additional products and services but all the intangibles and little things that together deliver exceptional service and a delightful customer experience.

Client behaviour is never linear and often unexpected so the key to success is to become more responsive to the actions that clients take. An obvious first step is therefore to ask for feedback. It seems such a simple action, yet so many organisations overlook it or believe that customers' comments are in some way not insightful.

Inevitably, the initial responses will be from avid if not 'professional' complainers but even this group should be listened to - complaints just as much as positive suggestions can provide a signpost to successful improvements.

One of the most valuable contributions will be generated by those that will need to be actively encouraged to comment. These are the customers who appear satisfied, because they do not express dissatisfaction directly to the firm. Nonetheless you can be sure some will experience dissatisfaction, and they will leave as soon as another comes up with a better offer. Making an effort to ask them about what they think can therefore stop potential deserters before it is too late to act. This sort of feedback does not have to be confined to organised questionnaires and research techniques. It can also be generated by the day-to-day interaction between customer and company.

Rubbing shoulders with existing customers and taking note of their spontaneous comments and behaviour, provides the chance to find out their motivations and attitudes which in turn can be turned into strategies to deliver customer satisfaction.

One partner reported that she found the feedback useful even from satisfied customers as it highlighted the need to add an additional question to her initial conversations with customers. e.g. *'How would you like me to communicate with you e.g. by mail, e-mail, fax etc.'*

Holding onto the notion that consumers will continue to buy out of loyalty ultimately means losing sight of real customers and they way they behave. But companies which are brave enough to see through this myth will be open to learning from their customers. If they can instill the kind of customer focus that originally made the business successful in the first place, they will attract and keep customers. They may never be loyal customers, but these companies will be able to keep retaining them year after year.

Our research and experience across many market sectors leads us to the belief that the individual or team that delivers the service should be the ones who ask the customer for feedback on how well they were doing. Surveys conducted by external agencies and non-line functions are okay however the results are at risk from being sanitised and watered down to a set of relatively meaningless generalisations displayed on colour coded charts. Real and instant change happens when the customer tells the service provider to their face what they think.

# 12: Training professionals to become Rainmakers

Our business has, for the most part, involved training, facilitating and coaching our clients. We were particularly interested to learn what firms are doing to increase the capability of their people.

Most stated that training was delivered in short seminars from one speaker to the next. Some speakers were good, some OK, many were very poor. Few had any structured sales development plans other than becoming qualified.

One senior partner told us that they recently had a seminar to learn how typical manufacturing worked and how directors made purchasing decisions. He told the tutor that it was the first non-legal course he had been on in the last 15 years. The fact that he thought the course was a waste of time was almost immaterial. It was the fact that the decision makers realised that the senior partners recognised that non-technical training was vital for the continued success of the business.

One representative of a big 4 accounting firm told us that he was amazed at the vast sums spent on expensive course in flashy hotels for the partners who did nothing different as a result. His view, rightly in our eyes, is that without someone to coach them to apply what they had learned the course would become yet another expensive set of course notes gathering dust on a shelf.

A great example of how training can be immense waste of time and effort was a conversation with an accountant at a networking event. She told us that she had recently been to a seminar on networking. She said it had been highly interactive and fun and there were many great ideas delivered by the trainer who, by the sounds of it, knew what he was talking about. She was observed at this networking lunch which was attended by around 150 local business executives. Her behaviour, we suspect, did not match what she had learned. For example:

- Once sat down she never moved from her seat
- She only spoke to the people who spoke to her first
- She did not create any interest in her business other than to say who they were and what they did
- She did not have any business cards with her to distribute
- Unless she had a photographic memory she did not take down any specific details of potential leads

We asked her how much of the training she had put into practice. Her response was a thank you for the reminder, she told us she would get the course notes out someday soon!

We strongly suspect she did not follow up any of the contacts and when asked by her boss how the event went she probably would have replied. *'It was a bit quiet, not much use really!'*

## 12.1 Great examples of approaches to training and coaching that deliver results

One of the best examples of a training/coaching programme for Rainmakers is a firm who had hired (after trying many options) an external agency to deliver a series of half-day workshops every two weeks/month to an 'intact' account team. This team were learning to work together to win large bids with new clients and to work more effectively to exploit incremental business opportunities within their existing accounts.

The trainers/coaches would deliver appropriate sales techniques and models dependent on where the team were in their development of the bid. The teams were then accountable for applying what they had learned over the next 2-4 weeks and reporting back to the coach at the next workshop. According to the interviewee this form of coaching was reaping significant rewards for the following reasons.

- o The participants dictated the agenda of what they wanted to learn.
- o The learning is tied to specific business-related objectives.

- It is a continuous process with the training delivered in bite-sized chunks over time.
- The training is delivered to a team who use the techniques delivered by the coaches to help them work more effectively together.
- The coach reinforces the techniques until they become embedded and 'the way we do things around here.'

Another firm told us how they were on the cusp of creating an army of
big-hitting Rainmakers. They were meticulous in their approach which involved, over a 12 to 18 month period, the following:

1. Employing an external agency with credibility to deliver a series of short, focused training workshops covering:

   - How people make decisions when purchasing professional services.
   - How to create interest in the customer's mind that you are worth talking to.
   - How to differentiate yourself.
   - How to understand the different types of customer.
   - How to create rapport.
   - How to create a customer relationship strategy.
   - How to measure and monitor touch points with the customer.
   - How to find good reasons to call people.
   - How to organise yourself.
   - How to use customer contact IT systems.

2. Getting the participants to set themselves a series of process and outcome goals including, for example; number of contacts required to get the first appointment, numbers of meetings with customers, number of meetings and other contacts required to close the sale, number of personal introductions as well as fees generated.

3. Running follow-up workshops using peer pressure to embed the behaviours taught on the training programme.

4. One-to-one coaching with the participants, irrespective of their ability or performance, to dramatically increase productivity.

5. Celebrating success and naming and shaming people who do not tow the line.

6. Measuring the Return on Investment to validate the added value from the training and coaching.

7. Repeating the whole process to develop the next generation of Rainmakers using successful people from the previous programme as coaches.

## 12.2 Busting some myths about coaching

We were surprised to learn that the decision makers in many accounting and law firms had not invested in either training their managers to coach their teams or external agencies to coach their fee earners. This is despite the overwhelming evidence across industry that demonstrates unequivocally that high quality coaching delivers results and that the discipline and practice of business coaching in the UK is increasing exponentially.

We discovered three reasons for the apparent lack of interest:

- Partners have not experienced high quality executive coaching and therefore cannot see the value in it.
- HR professionals and other decision makers believe that their lawyers and accountants will not readily take to it.
- Senior staff have heard about coaching through the grapevine and developed an unhealthy scepticism about coaching as a skill and/or profession.

Note: The third reason is not unsurprising since coaching has yet to mature as a profession and there are many people in the market professing to be coaches. Many of them we have met and, to be honest, wouldn't give them the time of day!

Interestingly, as a firm of experienced coaches, we are trained to spot instances where coaching is the most appropriate personal development process to deploy. It was absolutely clear to us that many of the respondents we interviewed were 'not in a good place' and would have valued an intimate dialogue with an experienced business coach.

In summary coaching is perfect for people who are short on time, quick thinking and want results fast.

In appendix 8 we have shared some of our views and beliefs about, what we call, 'Guerrilla coaching'.

# 13: Some special comments about (and from) the ladies

It was not an explicit intention of the research to explore any issues associated with gender. However, as stated elsewhere in the report, some of the ladies were frustrated by some of the male dominated macho attitudes in their firms.

Some of the younger women we interviewed and learned about were concerned about having to network on their own and the conclusions their colleagues and clients might incorrectly draw when mixing with people at dinners and lunches.

One hugely successful young male accountant, who ran a regional office of one of the top 10 accountancy firms, was delighted to hire an ambitious female executive. She quickly learned how to network successfully in the business clubs set up specifically for female business professionals. This became a lucrative source of new business contacts that could not have been opened up by any of the others in the business development team.

Sometimes during a research project we leave an interview absorbed and inspired from spending time with a lively, interesting and hugely entertaining professional. In this case we interviewed a serial networker who was tremendously well connected in her city having developed strong relationships with the movers and shakers in the area including the local media. It was easy to understand why she is so successful as she had the ability to instantly develop rapport with people.

However her success came with a price. It was clear that she believed some of her colleagues were envious of always seeing her name in the local press and various law journals. We asked her how this jealousy manifested itself. Her reply was the odd comment both in her presence and behind her back designed to undermine her. She had evidence to conclude that this was less about her success and more about her gender.

Whilst she had the strength of character to see these comments as petty jealousies, it is something that aspiring female Rainmakers may have to learn to handle.

# 14: Some tips for the smaller firms

One of the comments from a reader of the first draft report was that *"this will scare the pants off the smaller firms."* This is certainly not our intention, all we have done is report what we observed and were told. As a professional services firm grows it will undoubtedly come across some of the issues we have raised.

The only chapters that may have less validity for the smaller firms are 4,5,6 and 8. The remainder are all appropriate.

There are three additional lessons for the smaller firms.

1. Niche, niche, niche!

Undoubtedly one of the keys to becoming successful in any market is carving out a niche. Many of the most successful firms we spoke to had something they could use to differentiate themselves. Mostly it was a specific market sector that they could focus on and become experts in. At Bozeat Consulting we have focused Making it Rain on the legal, financial services and accounting professions. This makes it easier to learn the market, develop appropriate solutions and alert the attention of key influencers and decision makers.

2. Partner, partner, partner!

When the marketing budget is limited it is essential to form relationships with people who will become your advocates. Successful Rainmakers are habitual networkers who work extremely hard at building strong networks of advocates who are happy to recommend them to their colleagues, clients, friends and family. They work on the basis of 'givers gain' i.e. those who deliver more than is expected will inevitably reap the rewards.

3. Become a Guerilla Marketer

This term was released into the business world by Jay Conrad. Essentially Guerilla marketers use as many low cost routes to market as they can. Guerilla marketing is more about matching wits than matching budgets. Guerilla marketing can be as different from traditional marketing as guerilla warfare is from traditional warfare. Rather than marching their marketing budgets forth like infantry divisions, guerilla marketers snipe away with their marketing resources for maximum impact.

# 15: Can you learn to skate anti-clockwise?

Please pay particular attention when reading this chapter. It is the most important and potentially the most challenging to absorb.

It was one of those late night conversations with one of the most successful professional services entrepreneurs we know. In the late 90s Steve left an £80k annual salary plus perks to start his own financial services business. He has gone from 0 to 600 new customers in just 5 years and now works with just the top 20 clients who between them deliver 80% of his turnover. Steve realised as he approached his 40s that by 50 he was either going to be an inventor or work for one. He wisely became the former.

One of Steve's favourite lines is: *"People in the professional services need to learn how to skate anti-clockwise"*. In his opinion most accountants, solicitors and people in his own profession skate clockwise and herd with the pack just like everyone else. They have become conditioned to accept the norms and beliefs communicated by everyone else. Their paradigms (how they view the world) are just the same, the thinking is the same, the excuses for not doing things differently are the same and the results are more or less the same.

He recited a story from one of his customers, a millionaire property developer, who describes his accountants as *"Heinously boring and golden hearted, they deliver their work with military precision but not with their soul"*. His view is that the professions are run by professionals who aspire to be mavericks but daren't become one. His own favourite line is this: *"They are mavericks to the end of their shield."*

In business he asks his accountants not to be unethical or break the law; he just wants his partners to have life and be daring and fun to work with. The truth in his eyes is that everybody has something, however not everyone has the will to turn that something into something extraordinary.

This then is the final and ultimate paradox revealed in our research.

**People in the professional services want to be true to themselves at home and in business but very few have the courage to reveal their true selves to the world.**

Late nights bring great questions. We will finish this penultimate chapter with the questions we consider to be the most profound;

- Can you get to a place where every day in business you give all of your true self?
- When you get married and you ask your true friends to your wedding how many of them would be your customers? (If you already are married just use your imagination.)
- Can you get to a place where friendship supersedes business?
- How fast must you learn to skate anti-clockwise?

Note: By the way, whilst reading his chapter, if you have found yourself spending the majority of your time thinking about whether the majority of people on a skating rink skate clockwise or anti-clockwise you have entirely missed the point!

# 16: Final conclusions

When we set out on this journey to discover the factors that contributed to and inhibited sales success in professional service firms we had an idea what it would reveal. Some of our original thoughts were confirmed and there were many surprises. Here are our top 8 conclusions:

1. There are some fabulous examples of how professional service firms are blowing the competition away. If they can do it then anyone can, all it requires is an open mind, a willingness to model others and hard work.

2. There are some unhelpful beliefs amongst the professions that are preventing fee earners believing that they can become Rainmakers.

3. There are certain personality traits trained into people that both inhibit and promote Rainmaking behaviour.

4. Becoming a Rainmaker requires patience, discipline, hard work and a route map. The good news is that anyone can do it.

5. Now is certainly not the time to rest on your laurels, the industry is becoming ever more competitive and customer loyalty is increasingly becoming a thing of the past.

6. Coaching combined with training in proven techniques is the most effective personal development vehicle for generating exceptional results for fee earners who are short on time and require results fast.

7. Professional services firms must become more people oriented if they are to successfully create the next generation of Rainmakers.

8.  Budding Master Rainmakers must learn to skate anti-clockwise.

We'll leave the final words to W Edwards Deming and Charles Darwin.

**"It is not necessary to change. Survival is not mandatory."**
**W Edwards Deming**

**"It is not the strongest of the species that survives, nor the most intelligent. It is the one that is the most adaptable to change."**
**Charles Darwin**

# Appendix 1: Contributors/inhibitors to sales success in professional services businesses

**Note: if the appendixes are difficult to read for you then you can download a document containing them all from here** http://chilp.it/7c7844

The following tables are the preliminary findings of research conducted into the factors that contribute to and inhibit successful business development within a professional services partnership. You are invited to consider to what degree these factors and their implications apply to your organisation or organisations you have a relationship with. As you review the research please consider the priorities for your business.

Contributors to this preliminary research include BDO Stoy Hayward, Geldards LLP Solicitors, Millfield Financial Services and numerous individual contributions.

| Factor | Potential contributors to business development | Potential inhibitors to business development |
|---|---|---|
| Partnerships are often organised into a set of independent businesses with their own specific field of expertise. | <ul><li>Autonomy to 'do their own thing'</li><li>Entrepreneurial flare is encouraged</li><li>Strong focus on the subject matter and/or industry sector</li></ul> | <ul><li>Reluctance to share good practice with other partners</li><li>Inertia in creating uniform sales processes and approaches</li><li>Lack of co-ordinated sales approach between departments and offices</li><li>Protectionism over existing clients</li></ul> |
| Partners targeted and bonus paid on billable hours. | <ul><li>Opportunities for promotion</li><li>Significant rewards</li></ul> | <ul><li>As partners rise to the top there is little incentive to share sales opportunities unless there is a WIIFM (What's In It For Me)</li><li>Lack of incentive to sell</li><li>Reluctance to fully engage their own teams in selling activities</li></ul> |
| Partners and senior professionals have a significant degree of power and opportunities to influence senior people in the client organisation during a piece of work with a client. For example, during an audit. | <ul><li>Opportunities to build excellent relationships with senior people</li><li>Huge scope for identifying opportunities for incremental sales</li><li>Opportunity to assign a specific client liaison partner who has account management responsibilities</li></ul> | <ul><li>Potential for arrogance and patronising behaviour preventing listening</li><li>Not always spotting incremental sales opportunities</li><li>Disproportionate amount of time spent by liaison partners who engage in schmoozing activities that keep the customer happy at the detriment of pursuing new sales opportunities</li><li>Complacency, the work is coming in so why bother to sell?</li><li>Choosing an inappropriate person to be the account manager</li></ul> |

| | | |
|---|---|---|
| Accountants/lawyers/financial services professionals are experts in their field. | • Clearly defined and recognisable skills set<br><br>• Opportunities to prove their worth<br><br>• Clear career progression | • The profession can breed cautious behaviour<br><br>• Huge emphasis on technical knowledge and skills, less so on selling skills<br><br>• Difficult to change the mindset/identity of professional services people to become sellers<br><br>• Reluctance to highlight and share opportunities with others who may have the capability to fulfil a sales opportunity that is outside their own scope/capability<br><br>• Hesitancy to move into situations where their lack of skill/knowledge might be exposed |
| Tradition. | • Common practice is embedded into the culture of the profession | • Reluctance to take personal risks<br><br>• Fear resulting from having to meet new/senior people<br><br>• Difficult to change the mindset |
| New regulations, for example in accountancy, mean there are many opportunities for up-selling and cross-selling. | • Many opportunities for selling additional services<br><br>• Many opportunities for creating strategic alliances with people/organisations who have complementary products and services | • People becoming very possessive<br><br>• Fear of working with other people who they believe may 'cock up' the existing relationship<br><br>• Fear of 'letting go' and losing control of an account<br><br>• Fear that opportunities passed to others may not be reciprocated so why do it?' |

# Appendix 2: 30 key business development challenges facing professional service firms

These are the key business-related challenges revealed during an extensive survey of the top city and regional solicitors and accountancy practices in the UK. We have conducted a comprehensive research project in a highly successful law firm plus 31one-to-one interviews with partners, senior partners, heads of marketing, human resources professionals and fee earners representing over 40% of the top 30 accounting firms in the UK and one of the big 4.

In addition we interviewed a number of successful solicitors and professionals from related industries including financial services, marketing and architecture. They were all asked the question *"What are the factors that contribute to and inhibit sales success in your firm?"* The responses reveal a series of key challenges that professional service firms face.

Please use the document to audit your current practices and prioritise your business development activities.
You may like to use the following ratings as a guide.

| Rating | Meaning | Description |
|--------|---------|-------------|
| 5 | Outstanding | We consistently excel and can clearly differentiate ourselves from our competitors. |
| 4 | Good | We are doing almost all that we can. Some evidence of outstanding performance. |
| 3 | Average | We are doing what we can and we recognise there are large gaps in our performance |
| 2 | Below Ave | Some minor evidence of progress. Likely to cause significant problems if not addressed. |
| 1 | Poor | This is an area of genuine concern. |

Many of our clients prefer an **independent assessment** using this or other audit processes. This guarantees that the research **results are independent, accurate and valid**.

| No. | Description | Rating |
|-----|-------------|--------|
| 1 | How to create an environment where the fee earners, who are not performing to their potential, are consistently motivated to effectively market and sell themselves and the business. | |
| 2 | How to re-energise partners once they have 'made it' to want to re-engage in the volume and scope of rainmaking activities that allowed them to make it in the first place. | |
| 3 | How to effectively channel the activities of motivated and intelligent professionals to effectively sell themselves and the business. | |
| 4 | How to ensure all fee earners are equipped with the requisite knowledge and skills to be able to spot and capitalise on incremental business opportunities in existing accounts. | |
| 5 | How to create the conditions whereby fee earners are motivated to take the time to equip themselves with marketing and business development knowledge and skills. | |
| 6 | How to ensure fee earners adopt a rifle rather than a scatter gun approach to marketing and business development i.e. paying attention to a smaller number of targets. | |
| 7 | How to find ways for the fee earners to meet the customer to talk about what they want when they want and with whom they want. | |
| 8 | How to inspire the fee earners to consistently measure the 'cause and effect' of their rainmaking activity i.e. measure what they do vs the quantifiable results of their actions. | |
| 9 | How to 'wow' the client during a sales presentation. | |
| 10 | How to increase the level of individual responsibility and accountability of the fee earners. | |
| 11 | How to ensure the existing high-performing fee earners are actively engaged in developing the next generation of rainmakers. | |
| 12 | How to maintain a healthy balance between rainmaking activities that are outside of normal working hours and home life. | |
| 13 | How to ensure the methods by which the firm sells and markets itself are adapted to suit the female fee earners. | |
| 14 | How to engage the entire workforce to believe in their own ability to sell themselves and the firm and become active | |

| | | |
|---|---|---|
| | marketeers. | |
| 15 | How to create the conditions whereby the fee earners open their minds to accept, practice and adopt working practices that are proven to deliver outstanding results. | |
| 16 | How to ensure the fee earners continuously improve as a direct result of proactively listening to and acting on the customers' perceptions of the quality of service they deliver. | |
| 17 | How to capture and analyse information emanating from conversations between the fee earners and customers in order to make strategic decisions regarding the future of the business. | |
| 18 | How to ensure the fee earners are consistently sharing good practice and sales opportunities with colleagues i.e. moving from *"my customer"* to *"our customer."* | |
| 19 | In the larger firms: how to eradicate any 'silo mentality' and organise the business into client-focused sales and service teams. | |
| 20 | How to ensure the fee earners build mutually rewarding relationships with partner firms in order to develop and capitalise on business development opportunities. | |
| 21 | How to ensure the fee earners consistently behave in a manner that positively differentiates themselves and the firm from the competition. | |
| 22 | How to package services so that they make sense to the client, enable the client to see what value the services will deliver and demonstrate how the firm differentiates itself from the competition. | |
| 23 | How to balance fostering an entrepreneurial spirit in the fee earners with consistent adherence to the firm's business development and marketing processes. | |
| 24 | How to ensure the support teams in marketing, HR and business development have the credibility, skill and power to influence the fee earners. | |
| 25 | How to align the partners to a common set of principles, values and behaviours that foster continued business development and success. | |
| 26 | How to ensure that the motivated, intelligent and successful rainmakers are excellent role models. | |
| 27 | How to create a feedback culture where all staff welcome, receive and act on expertly delivered feedback from their | |

| | | |
|---|---|---|
| | colleagues. | |
| 28 | How to create a creative, hard-working and entrepreneurial place to work whilst respecting the confidential nature of the business. | |
| 29 | How to protect the workforce by skillfully and sensitively disengaging senior fee earners from management activities and duties that they are uncomfortable with, unsuitable for or unwilling to carry out. | |
| 30 | How to turn exceptional professional services practitioners into inspirational leaders. | |

# Appendix 3: 11 options for creating the next generation of Rainmakers

## Overview

Following the research, we have compiled a series of options to enable a professional services firm to rapidly accelerate its business success. On the following pages there are 11 alternatives that can be used in isolation or in association with others.

Together they will deliver quick wins in business development whilst ensuring the continued success of the business by addressing the change and cultural issues. Please note that some of the options are designed for larger firms. The options are designed to achieve one or more of the following:

- Changing the culture of the business to break down the silo mentality to become more inclusive
- Equipping the next generation of Master Rainmakers
- Creating a feedback culture
- Making people accountable for their actions
- Turning managers into inspirational leaders
- Increasing the volume and quality of business development/marketing activity in order to win business with new customers
- Ensuring everyone in the business fully understands the true capability of the firm and works together irrespective of their position or discipline to deliver exceptional service and move 'wider and deeper' in accounts

# The options:

| Option | Description |
|---|---|
| 1 | Conduct an extensive independent survey within the firm using the 30 challenges and related behaviours. |
| 2 | Continue the process of changing the culture of the business by defining and creating consensus around the culture it wants to create. |
| 3 | Deliver the change the business requires through focused high performance teams. |
| 4 | Engage teams of partners, junior partners and support staff to find the best way to exploit the potential in existing accounts and/or break into new markets/customers. |
| 5 | Coach the coach – a specific programme of activities to help managers bring the best out of their people. |
| 6 | Creation and delivery of a 12 to 18-month leadership and/or sales development journey. |
| 7 | One-to-one executive 'Guerrilla' coaching. |
| 8 | Coaching the Master Rainmakers to pass on their skills and knowledge to the next generation. |
| 9 | Creation of a Master Rainmaker's benchmark. |
| 10 | Inspire everyone in the firm to become a marketeer. |
| 11 | Front line people conduct a Customer Review Dialogue (CRD) process. |

| Option 1 | | |
| --- | --- | --- |
| **Conduct an extensive independent survey within the firm using the 30 challenges and related behaviours** | | |
| **Approach** | **Techniques** | **Key Performance Indicators** |
| • An independent survey based on the 30 business development challenges.<br><br>• The survey is conducted at all levels: partner, junior partner and support staff. | • Paper-based/electronic survey.<br><br>• One-to-one interviews.<br><br>• Focus groups.<br><br>• Live observation. | • Completion of the survey.<br><br>• Revelation of the priorities for the business agreed by all the key stakeholders.<br><br>• Compilation of objective and subjective data. |

**Benefits**

- Creates alignment between the key stakeholders regarding the priorities for the business.
- Independence ensures all the issues are revealed.
- The results create a compelling argument to create the momentum for change.
- During the process of conducting the research people who are surveyed often become advocates to the changes brought in by the business.
- Data can be used to measure trends in the future.

| Option 2 | | |
|---|---|---|
| Continue the process of changing the culture of the firm by defining and creating consensus around the culture the leadership wants to create | | |
| **Approach** | **Techniques** | **Key Performance Indicators** |
| • 1.5 to 2 day workshop with the management board.<br><br>• Subsequent workshops with the partners and junior staff to generate consensus.<br><br>• Defined process to define the firm's vision, values and behaviours. | • Examples from organisations who have used values and behaviour to deliver change.<br><br>• Facilitated process. | • Agreement to the firm's mission, vision and values.<br><br>• Agreement to the KPIs and measures of success.<br><br>• Fee earners recognising the need to change and take the initial steps to do so. |

**Benefits**

- Creates alignment between the stakeholders in the business.

- Extremely motivating.

- Places values and behaviour clearly on peoples' radar.

- Defines the behaviours which will become the way we want to be.

- The values and behaviours form the basis of competency assessment and reward .

- This will cause people to look in the mirror and ask themselves how they need to change.

- The values and behaviours form part of the recruitment criteria.

- Breaks down the silo-mentality.

- Essential to do if long term success is to be maintained.

- The result of the workshops will be commitment to the plans required to drive the business forward.

| Option 3 | | |
| --- | --- | --- |
| **Deliver the change the business requires through focused high performance teams** | | |
| **Approach** | **Techniques** | **Key Performance Indicators** |
| <ul><li>Invite/nominate high-flying partners and/or potential partners to form teams who will drive the change agenda.</li><li>Each team will have a specific project outcome and are sponsored by a management board member.</li><li>Teams will meet regularly, at least once a month initially, in a facilitated/coaching workshop.</li><li>Work on the project will take place between the workshops.</li></ul> | <ul><li>7-step change project process.</li><li>Talents of a change agent e.g.<ul><li>Change beam.</li><li>Change curve.</li><li>Stakeholder analysis.</li><li>4-MAT.</li><li>SPPEV.</li><li>3 times convincer.</li><li>WIIFM v WAMI.</li></ul></li></ul> | <ul><li>Achievement of the project outcomes based on key business imperatives and within defined timescales.</li><li>Culture affected permanently and for the better.</li><li>Agreement to key performance indicators.</li></ul> |

**Benefits**

- Each of the change issues have been identified in the research. These teams will address them.
- Alignment of the partners as the teams will need to gain commitment to their plans.
- Empowered people making genuine change, future leaders have the opportunity to shine.
- Change from within rather than driven top-down.
- Realisation of key business deliverables.
- Tools are delivered at the right time to be applied immediately.
- Knowledge is pooled and shared.
- Breaks down functional silos by causing people to work together effectively.
- Controllable.
- Action plans drawn up, teams are committed to making them happen.
- Short focused workshops to minimise disruption to the participant's normal work.

| Option 4 Engage teams of partners, junior partners and support staff to find the best way to exploit the potential in existing accounts and/or break into new markets/customers | | |
| --- | --- | --- |
| **Approach** | **Techniques** | **Key Performance Indicators** |
| • Teams meet regularly, initially at least once a month in a series of facilitated workshops with a specific business development agenda.<br><br>• The team will define the size and scope of the sales opportunity and how they intend to exploit it.<br><br>• The team's progress will be monitored over time. | The participants are introduced to a suite of simple yet powerful tools to manage accounts. These include:<br><br>• The 7 habits of highly effective account managers<br><br>• Protecting your position within the customer<br><br>• Internal networking processes<br><br>• PI techniques<br><br>• Marketing techniques | • Uncovering of new business opportunities.<br><br>• Winning new and incremental business. |
| **Benefits**<br><br>• Realisation of specific business development activities.<br><br>• Introduction of powerful sales techniques delivered 'just-in-time' for the teams to use them.<br><br>• Fee earners become used to working together within tightly controlled conditions and will get used to reporting on progress using standard reporting protocols.<br><br>• There is no wasted time teaching tools that the participants will not use.<br><br>• Workshops are short to ensure time away from fee-earning work is limited.<br><br>• Fee earners are forced to work together to break down any existing silo mentality.<br><br>• The participants can see the WIIFM and will be motivated to be successful. | | |

**Option 5**

**Coach the coach – a specific programme of activities to help managers bring the best out of their people**

| Approach | Techniques | Key Performance Indicators |
|---|---|---|
| • Selected partners are invited to participate in a series of assessment/developme nt activities to learn how to become effective coaches. | • G.R.O.W.<br>• Skill vs Will<br>• Situational leadership<br>• Confronting resistance and tackling interference<br>• 7-4-1 goal setting<br>• Understanding values | • Increase in the number and quality of performance related discussions.<br>• Completed personal development plans. |

**Benefits**

- Delivery of tangible benefits to both individuals and organisations.
- Very motivating for managers who acquire the ability to diagnose performance-related situations.
- An effective way to promote learning in the business.
- Coaching and mentoring are key mechanisms for transferring the learning from training back to the workforce.
- When coaching is managed effectively it can have a positive impact on the bottom line.
- The most powerful way to bring the best out of people.

| Option 6 | | |
|---|---|---|
| **Creation and delivery of a 12 to 18- month leadership and/or sales development journey** | | |
| **Approach** | **Techniques** | **Key Performance Indicators** |
| • Definition and delivery of a leadership journey for the partners, junior partners and senior support staff.<br><br>• Partners are assessed on their performance pre and post journey.<br><br>• The participants receive one-to-one coaching either from an external coach or a trained partner and/or they engage in peer coaching discussions.<br><br>• Journeys are tailored to various groups within the organisation.<br><br>• e.g. Fast track for senior managers and fundamentals for junior staff.<br><br>Notes:<br>Some pre-workshop reading may be required.<br><br><br><br><br>Sales and leadership journeys typically follow shortly after the mission, vision and values workshops in order to maintain and sustain momentum. | A series of leadership modules that typically include:<br><br>• Mindset.<br>• Coaching.<br>• Leading change.<br>• Meetings.<br>• Delegation.<br>• Empowerment.<br>• Inspirational leadership.<br>• Persuasive presenting.<br>• Handling difficult people.<br><br>Also there may be a series of Fast-Track Workshops to equip the leadership with the tools to coach their teams. Techniques covered may include:<br><br>• Speed stuns.<br>• Alternative timings.<br>• Disorientating the customer's expectations.<br>• Positive language.<br>• Powerful customer meetings.<br><br><br>• Handling inbound/outbound calls.<br>• Power agendas.<br>• Gatekeeper tools.<br>• Consultative selling.<br>• Negotiation.<br>• Account Management.<br>• Applied NLP – rapport building and eliciting the customers' values.<br>• PI techniques. | • Full and active participation.<br><br>• Application of the techniques.<br><br>• Visible and positive shift in the culture of the business. |
| **Benefits** | | |

- Immersion in techniques, all participants receive them simultaneously.
- A process to align the partners.
- Actual work is completed during the workshops.
- Peer coaching is used to ensure the participants share their issues and engage in problem solving activities.
- Silos permanently broken down.

**Option 7**
**One-to-one executive 'Guerrilla' coaching**

| Approach | Techniques | Key Performance Indicators |
|---|---|---|
| • This is used with specific people who have the potential to significantly increase their performance and require support to accelerate their development. <br><br> • Engagement typically begins with a three-way conversation with the participant, his/her sponsor and the coach. <br><br> • The executive coach will work with the individual typically for 6 to 12 months beginning with a one-day or half-day workshop followed by a series of telephone and/or face-to-face conversations. <br><br> Note: <br> One-to-one executive coaching is often an integral part of a 12 to 18 month development journey. | • Psychometric tools. <br> • Values and beliefs. <br> • Personal development plan. <br> • 7-4-1 goal setting. <br> • Building commitment. <br> • Reporting to include wins, challenges and actions. <br> • Overcoming personal interference. | • These are based on the performance objectives agreed at the outset with the sponsor and participant. |

**Benefits**
- People take individual responsibility for their development.
- Reduction in the financial cost of poor performance.
- A popular development mechanism and feature of a modern organisation.
- Supports other learning and development activities.
- Suits employees demand for different delivery mechanisms.
- Satisfies and prompts the need for lifelong development.
- Improved decision making by senior executives.
- Targeted 'just-in-time' development.
- Short, timely and focused coaching discussions.

| Option 8 | | |
| :-- | :-- | :-- |
| **Coaching the Master Rainmakers to pass on their skills and knowledge to the next generation** | | |
| **Approach** | **Techniques** | **Key Performance Indicators** |
| • Selected 'Master Rainmakers' are invited to participate in a series of development activities to equip them with the mindset and skills to coach others to become Rainmakers. | • Train-the-trainer.<br>• Persuasive presentations.<br>• Facilitation skills.<br>• Coaching techniques. | • Increase in the number of coaching workshops.<br>• Increase in the number and quality of coaching discussions.<br>• Increase in performance of the Rainmakers being coached. |

**Benefits**

- Delivery of tangible benefits to both individuals and organisations
- Very motivating for the Master Rainmakers who learn how to effectively accelerate the growth of the next generation of Rainmakers
- A strong message is sent to the organisation that coaching is the way forward
- An effective way to promote learning in the firm
- When coaching is managed effectively it can have a positive impact on the bottom line
- The most powerful way to bring the best out of people

**Option 9**
**Creation of a Master Rainmaker's benchmark**

| Approach | Techniques | Key Performance Indicators |
|---|---|---|
| • Selected 'Master Rainmakers' are invited to develop a benchmark for what they do, think and believe that makes them effective in winning business. | • A series of interviews and/or facilitated workshops to draw out the key attributes and behaviours of the high producing partners. | • Completed benchmark.<br>• Widespread use in assessment and monitoring activities. |

**Benefits**

- Capture of intellectual capital.

- A 'no argument' document that demonstrates how to win new and incremental business.

- The process will gain commitment from the partners and junior partners to help them understand what they must do to be successful.

- The benchmark will become an essential aid in coaching discussions.

| Option 10 | | |
| --- | --- | --- |
| **Inspire everyone in the firm to become a marketeer** | | |
| **Approach** | **Techniques** | **Key Performance Indicators** |
| • A series of coaching workshops designed to equip the participants with the 'skill and will' to sell the firm's services.<br><br>• The coaching is mutually supported by the introduction of systems and processes to reward success.<br><br>• Communication activities to ensure all the team have the knowledge to effectively sell the firm.<br><br>• Measurement of the volume and quality of PIs and the resulting business. | • Consultative selling.<br><br>• Creating hooks that entice potential clients.<br><br>• The 'Accomplished Networker' training programme.<br><br>• 'Internal PI (personal introduction) Exchange'.<br><br>• Team-based working. | • Increase in sales activity.<br><br>• Increase in the volume and quality of leads and PIs.<br><br>• Increase in business won.<br><br>• Higher morale and energy. |

**Benefits**

- Improvement in cross-departmental communication.
- Dormant talent realised and developed.
- Fun!
- Higher volume and quality of leads.
- Increase in morale.
- People who are continuously learning and thirsty for knowledge and skills are more productive.
- Empowered people.

| Option 11 | | |
|---|---|---|
| **Front line people conduct a Customer Review Dialogue (CRD) process** | | |
| **Approach** | **Techniques** | **Key Performance Indicators** |
| • A systematic series of interviews by front line people with key customers to ascertain their level of satisfaction with the service they receive.<br><br>• Data from the interviews is compiled to reveal a S.W.O.T. analysis as perceived by the customer.<br><br>• This analysis becomes the catalyst for change in the business. | • Interview techniques e.g<br>  ○ Listening<br>  ○ Asking probing questions<br>  ○ Resolving problems<br>  ○ Commitment to action | • S.W.O.T. analysis by individual customer, customer groups and the whole business.<br><br>• Robust individual, department and company performance improvement plans. |

**Benefits**

- Front line fee earners and support staff are engaged in one-to-one dialogues with customers.
- Accountability for improving customer service rests with the front line.
- Excitement and motivation derived from an in depth understanding of the customer's needs.
- Management have holistic and accurate view of how well they are perceived by customers.
- Results of the CRD process often augment the company's business plan.
- Results of the CRD sets a benchmark for where the business is now and where it wants to be. A second CRD process after 9 to 12 months will measure improvement.
- Highlighting of further business opportunities that may not have surfaced without the dialogue.

# Appendix 4: Making the time to do what needs to be done

We once overheard a trainer say to her participants in a workshop *"time is money."* A rather smart participant responded *"I'm not sure I agree. Time is everything."* It is difficult to disagree.

To realise the value of ONE YEAR, ask a student who failed their exams.

To realise the value of ONE MONTH, ask a mother who gave birth to a premature baby.

To realise the value of ONE WEEK, ask the editor of a weekly newspaper.

To realise the value of ONE HOUR, ask two lovers who are waiting to meet.

To realise the value of ONE MINUTE, ask a person who missed the plane.

To realise the value of ONE SECOND, ask a person who just avoided an accident.

To realise the value of ONE THOUSANDTH OF A SECOND, ask the person who won a silver medal in the Olympics.

These are 8 proven techniques for managing time:

1. Give precise times for how long you are going to spend on a specific activity and stick to it
2. Distinguish between urgent and important tasks
3. Book yourself time in the diary to do the most important things
4. Learn to say no (sensitively of course)
5. Only do the most important things
6. Plan your diary at least 6 months ahead

7. Reward yourself for finishing work ahead of time
8. Go home!

And finally the best technique of all:

At the end of every day, write down everything you are going to do the next day and in order of priority. Start the next day with item 1and work through the list until the list is finished. Do this for 30 days until it becomes a habit. Then, if you have people working for you, persuade them to do the same.

# Appendix 5: 10 steps to transform your organisation

This experience reveals the 10 steps proven to deliver change irrespective of what the change is, the nature of the business and how many people are impacted. A note of caution, skipping or not following through fully on a step creates an illusion of speed but comes back to haunt you later.

| Step | Activity | Description |
|------|----------|-------------|
| 1 | Have a compelling reason to change | This includes defining and communicating the depth, breadth and implications of the pain that exists in the organisation. |
| 2 | Pull a powerful team together | No change happens unless there is a team of committed, influential and skilled 'pioneers' who have the authority and support from the top to deliver the change agenda. |
| 3 | Create a compelling picture of the new world | The people affected by the change need to know where the future lies and crucially what's in it for them. |
| 4 | Do some modeling and develop a flexible, integrated plan | Just about anything a business wants to do has been done by someone somewhere else. This step involves benchmarking and adopting, adapting and installing new ways of working. |
| 5 | Ensure that those armed with the change agenda are capable of delivery | Change agents need to be equipped with a range of skills to engage the hearts and minds of the people whose commitment is necessary for the change to be delivered. |
| 6 | Communicate, communicate, communicate! | Most change programmes are grossly under communicated. This step involves regular bulletins, workshops, road shows and the use of every media and communication channel available. |
| 7 | Expect that obstacles | Redundant systems and organisation structures |

| | | |
|---|---|---|
| | will occur and be prepared to remove them! | will need to be changed or removed. Leaders will need to 'change the people or change the people.' |
| 8 | Manufacture some early wins | Large change projects begin with small and early wins. Resources are directed to ensuring a win takes place that is directly attributable to the change effort. Success is celebrated and widely communicated. |
| 9 | Maintain momentum | Early wins breed the confidence necessary to take on bigger challenges and bigger egos! |
| 10 | Ensure that the changes become embedded into the culture | This involves writing procedures so that things that were once new are now 'the way we do things around here.' |

# Appendix 6: Preparing for a meeting

It has been proven that the consistent use of proven meetings skills and techniques can reduce the average length of meetings by at least a half while increasing the output by at least 100%.

Here is a simple checklist for preparing for a meeting.

- Does the meeting purpose and agenda look and sound exciting to the participants?
- Have you started with the end in mind and considered in detail what the outcome(s) of the meeting should be?
- Have you enrolled the key players to ensure they are fully prepared for what is going to happen before, during and after the meeting?
- Does everyone understand what their role is in making the meeting a success?
- Have you prepared all the materials and equipment prior to the meeting?
- Have you chosen the best meeting processes to deliver the outcomes you want e.g. brainstorming, open forum, structured problem solving etc
- Does the meeting have a structure that will keep everyone engaged?
- Are you geared up to ensure that any documentation and minutes created at the meeting are delivered to the participants before they leave or very shortly after the meeting finishes?
- Have you a list of meeting ground rules that everyone adheres to

# Appendix 7: The Seven behaviours of high performing account managers

Shared use of these behaviours will dramatically increase the ability of account teams to work effectively together.

| Habit | Meaning |
|---|---|
| 1) Big Picture | Top Account Mangers are able to work at both the detail/operational and high levels keeping a 'helicopter view' on the account. |
| 2) Entry Strategies | Account Managers have to be able to see the people they want to see when they need to see them. This habit is concerned with getting into an account and navigating between decision makers, influencers and operators. |
| 3) Relationships | *'Relationships are everything in every business.'* It is crucial to build long-term relationships with the key players in accounts. |
| 4) Stakeholder Alignment | Top account managers need to make a series of interventions to cause those who hold the power in an account to align themselves with the proposed strategy. The successful account manager becomes a 'conductor of a human orchestra.' |
| 5) Spotting and creating opportunities | This habit means uncovering and developing opportunities that add value to the customer which more often than not will involve selling additional products or services. |
| 6) Differentiation | Any leading organisation has the ability to differentiate itself both from the products and services it offers and how its representatives behave. This habit examines how the account manager creates uniqueness in the eyes of the customer. |
| 7) Working the net Sharing | Top account managers are habitual networkers. They use their existing network of contacts to put them in touch with the people they want to do business with. |

# Appendix 8: Guerrilla coaching

Imagine that you decide you want to get yourself fit and that the gym is the right place to get in shape. You choose to hire a personal trainer to increase the probability that you will follow through on your great intentions.

What are the characteristics you will be looking for in this trainer? Probably some or all of the following:

- She has 'been there done that and got several T-shirts!'
- She is inspirational
- She is totally focused on you
- She spends time understanding your goals and crucially the motivation behind them
- She helps you break down the big goals into a series of achievable steps that stretch you
- She ensures that when one goal is reached the bar is set a little higher
- She is demanding, does not tolerate excuses and works you to your limit during the time you are with her
- She helps you keep track of progress to ensure you are following through on your great intentions when you are not with her
- She keeps you motivated even when the going gets tough
- She is flexible in her approach and finds new and innovative ways to help you meet your goals
- She celebrates your success
- You know she has done her job when you realise you would not have achieved as much without her help

This is exactly what a 'Guerrilla coach' does but in business.

The truth is we all coach all of the time. Every conversation we have is an opportunity to coach.

This is our definition of Guerrilla coaching.

*'Guerrilla coaches are proactive people who do whatever it takes to cause people to take extraordinary action in pursuit of worthy goals and aspirations'.*

Guerrilla coaches have the following beliefs:

- Everyone who they have the privilege to coach has a vast reservoir of talent and potential just waiting to be unleashed. The coach helps the coachee unlock it.
- Coaches are a source of inspiration to cause the coachee to have the self-motivation to do whatever it takes to get the job done.
- Coaches will use a wide variety of techniques to bypass and break through self-doubt or 'personal interference.'
- Coaches are both empathetic and demanding.
- Coaching requires resilience, an eye for detail, an open mind, patience, an unwavering focus on the individual and getting results.
- Coaches recognise that success is 80% mindset and 20% skills and knowledge.

Guerrilla Coaches are coached by their own Guerrilla Coaches.

# Appendix 9: The Customer Review Dialogue

## Introduction

In an age where customer satisfaction is used in the same breath as bottom line results, it is vital that business leaders implement ways of measuring how their customers perceive the service they provide. Feedback from customers is essential to ensure all front-line people continuously focus on what the customer wants in order to continually improve the quality of the service they deliver.

The objective of most businesses is to create committed customers. The greatest indicator of commitment is repeat business and increased repeat business. In **professional service businesses reputation counts for almost everything.** We do, however, live in an extremely competitive business environment and nothing can be taken for granted - even the most loyal customers can leave.
Therefore it is essential to continuously listen, learn and respond to your customers.

Searching for, listening to and acting on customers' feedback is important for six primary reasons:

1. It sends a message to customers that **their opinions are valued**
2. It demonstrates your willingness to **listen and respond** to their needs
3. It is an opportunity to **keep in touch**
4. It often reveals additional **sales opportunities**
5. It provides information to **enhance the way you work together**
6. It **prevents complacency**

This is sensible practice but evidence suggests that few organisations:

- have the right tools and techniques to gather customer feedback
- have a methodology for measuring and monitoring the quality of relationships with the customer
- can say they accurately understand their customers' requirements
- provide frequent and quality customer feedback to their employees

# The problem with surveys

There are many approaches for obtaining feedback. These include ad hoc conversations, questionnaires, focus groups and telephone surveys. All have their value yet in many organisations they do not always prompt positive action, often quite the reverse.

There are many reasons why traditional processes don't deliver:

1. Surveys often yield **poor return rates** and respondents are normally either **fans or gripers** and not the middle range of mildly satisfied/dissatisfied customers.
2. Anonymous surveys often lead to **defensive responses** from employees e.g. *'who said that?'* and *'what do you mean?'*
3. The measurement process focuses on getting a response about subjects that the supplier wants to explore **instead of the priorities of the customers.**
4. Insufficient people from across the organisation are involved in the development and delivery of the customer satisfaction measurement process. Rather it is **held in the domain of non-line functions** e.g. quality, HR, marketing, communications or business development or even external organisations.
5. The results of the surveys are **collated, aggregated, prioritised and sanitised** into a generic set of results which often hold **little meaning** for those who are supposed to take action as a result.
6. The results are distributed from the management layers to the front line. It is then incumbent upon the **management to drive action** through their people.
7. The systems often only **measure high-level issues** that front-line people cannot readily identify with.
8. The time taken from the start of the measurement process to the delivery of the results to running meetings to discuss what to do and then taking action may be so long that people can **lose sight of the urgency to do something** about the results.

The effect of these is that **front-line people can distance themselves** from the results and fail to accept ownership of the issues highlighted by the customers. Indeed it may be that they themselves are part of the problem.

Also, it is easy for people to adopt a **defensive stance** and blame others. The result is that people are **not galvanised into taking positive action**, which of course is the intent behind measuring customer satisfaction in the first place.

From the customer's point of view, if they are asked for feedback they want to feel confident that it will be acted upon swiftly and not lost into some bureaucratic black hole. It is crucial for those engaged in implementing the customer satisfaction measurement processes to be empowered do what is necessary almost at the point the feedback is solicited.

## The ingredients of an effective customer satisfaction measurement system

Experience suggests that the following ingredients are necessary if a customer satisfaction measurement system is to be successful:

- It must be tied directly to the **objectives and values** of the business.
- As many people in the organisation, including wherever appropriate the customer, are involved in its **conception, design and delivery.**
- It must be **simple, detailed and understandable** so those who are responsible for the service can take action.
- It must be **conducted frequently enough** to measure trend data.
- It should involve those who provide the service talking direct to the customer about a) **what is most important to them** and b) **how well they currently conform to their expectations.**
- It must enable people at the front line to take any **appropriate and instant action.**

- Data from a dialogue between front line people and the customer should be **collated into management information** to form an overall picture of how the organisation is performing.

Altogether this is a bottom-up, manageable and highly effective process. A process that places the ownership for the results and therefore accountability for addressing the resulting issues firmly with those who are responsible for providing the service.

The following diagram illustrates how the Customer review Dialogue works.
Initially the leadership decides what it wants to measure in terms of how they would like to be perceived by the customer. A list of customers is then compiled. The front line people are then trained to conduct the interviews who then arrange and conduct a Customer Review Dialogue with the nominated customers.
They record both what is important to the customer and critically how the customer rates the quality of service they receive.

The data is collected into a report which reveals a SWOT analysis of the business as seen by the customer. This is fed back to the leadership who translate the information into short-term actions and medium to long-term business strategy.
Finally the process is repeated after 9 to 12 months to measure improvements.

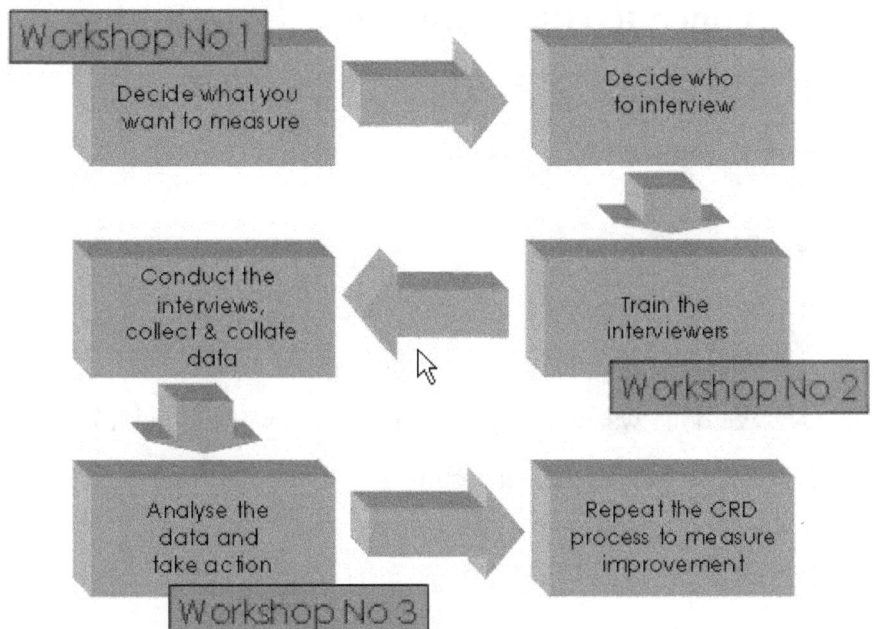

# Appendix 10: About Bozeat Consulting

**We are a training and coaching company...**

- We don't do soft skills
- We don't hug trees
- We don't believe training is always the answer
- We don't waste time your time or ours working with you unless we can deliver results

**However...**

**We do guarantee outstanding results by inspiring and coaching people to embrace the habits of top class professionals.**

For more details on how we can help you create the next generation of Rainmakers please explore our comprehensive websites www.bozeatconsulting.co.uk , www.simonbozeat.com and/or contact us:

Prospect House

Chapel Street

Oakthorpe

Derbyshire

DE12 7QT

Email:          simon@simonbozeat.com

# About The Author

A graduate from Nottingham University Simon Bozeat first worked for The Ford Motor Company and later found himself in training and personal development subsequently holding senior positions in Lloyds, Siemens and GEC

During the 90's Simon worked with the best of the best in training. Companies such as Huthwaite Research, PE International and PTP training and marketing

Simon became an expert in Behaviour Analysis. he learned the behaviours that distinguish the top performers from the average, He also learned NLP via Tony Robbins

Simon found that executives, managers, sales and non-operations support staff often lacked one core skill, **the ability to persuade other people to want what they want.**

Consequently the first suite of Simon's training products became known as **'Persuading Powerful People'.**

In 1997 Simon launched his own business and his first major client was Rolls-Royce Aerospace based in Derby. The initial contract was for 6 months however it went on for 3.5 years. Simon is now a genuine authority on how to make colossal change happen.

Simon became know in Rolls Royce as 'Mr Facilitator'. Whenever a senior executive needed to bring people together to address challenging problems then Simon was called in as the man to make it happen. He is a world-class facilitator skilled in bringing people together with well-intentioned yet disparate thoughts to align them around a compelling vision of the future and route map to make it happen.

It was during this period that, without knowing it, he became a one-to-one business coach. With so much experience to draw on Simon can rapidly help talented, ambitious and time-poor business professionals address complex change and persuasion related challenges.

At the dawn of the new millennium Simon turned his attention to the professional services market and the sales challenges they faced. He spent 6 months interviewing many of the UK's leading law, accounting firms and banks. He asked one question: "What are the factors which contribute to and hinder sales success in your business?" The result is the acclaimed white paper. 'Making it Rain, how to skate anti-clockwise' and a host of opportunities followed training people to sell, persuade and influence

Towards the end of the first decade of the 21st century Simon spotted a gap in the market for high profile business clubs. He launched the Ashby Business Club in 2008 which morphed into the Midlands Leadership Experience (MLE) in 2010.

Simon took advantage of 2012, the incredible year of sport in the UK, to become a triathlete. He is currently writing a book about the experience called 'Tri'ing to get in shape, one lampost at a time' He is raising considerable funds for his nominated charities whilst training to increase his distances with an ambition to complete an Ironman triathlon.

# Further Information

Working The Net: A practical Guide to Business Networking – Simon Bozeat 2013

How to Build a Profitable Business Network – Simon Bozeat Video Training

http://simonbozeat.com

If you enjoyed this book please leave a positive review on Amazon.com